UNMASKING
the Truth about
THAT DAY!

UNMASKING
the Truth about
THAT DAY!

*A thought-provoking and scriptural examination
of the most difficult and controversial topics
in the book of Revelation.*

Cathy R. Howe

XULON PRESS ELITE

Xulon Press Elite
2301 Lucien Way #415
Maitland, FL 32751
407.339.4217
www.xulonpress.com

Printed in the United States of America.

Paperback ISBN-13: 978-1-6628-1003-9
Ebook ISBN-13: 978-1-6628-1004-6

Preface

Throughout the ages, God has used unusual individuals to do his work. I think I am one of those *unusual*, but called, individuals. I am not a theologian. I have no influence over a large body of people. I cannot stand toe to toe with any great writers, but I believe I was called by God to write this book. I did not write it according to any exceptional talent, intelligence, or experience that I possess. I may not be able to answer a vast array of high-level theological challenges that may follow. I simply wrote this book to pass along what I have received from God in my study and meditation of his Word, particularly the book of Revelation. I desire to create a link in the chain of impact that *all* faithful and obedient saints have here on earth. When we obey God, we are but potter's clay, for the Master's purposes.

My hope is that the reader will gain a better understanding of *prophetic timing*, and the *mission* of God in *this millennium*, as it was taught by Christ and His disciples to the early Church. I hope to help readers see what God has been doing, and *is going to do*, through the body of Christ, from creation to the final symbolic last "day" at the second coming of Christ.

So why does this matter? Perhaps sooner than later, the faithful followers of Jesus Christ will be entering a time of great peril. We are living on the very threshold of when we will be the *key characters* in the days of the tribulation. We will not escape the hardships that are coming on the earth, but faithful followers of Jesus Christ are *assured* that the Spirit of God will be with us all the way to the glorious rapture of the Church, immediately *after* the symbolic seven-year tribulation. Persecution is not abnormal for Christ-followers. It is the standard.

> **1 Peter 4:12** Beloved, think it not strange concerning the *fiery trial* which is to try you, as though some strange thing happened unto you:

> **2 Timothy 3:12** Yea, and *all* that will live godly in Christ Jesus shall suffer persecution.

> **Philippians 1:29** For unto you it is given in the behalf of Christ, not only to believe on him, but also **to suffer** for his sake;

> **Matthew 5:10–12** Blessed are they which are persecuted for righteousness' sake: for theirs is the kingdom of heaven. Blessed are ye, when men shall revile you, and persecute you, and shall say all manner of evil against you falsely, for my sake. Rejoice, and be exceeding glad: for great is your reward in heaven: for so persecuted they the prophets which were before you.

> **1 Peter 4:13** But rejoice, inasmuch as ye are partakers of Christ's sufferings; that, when his glory shall be revealed, ye may be glad also with exceeding joy.

James 1:2 Count it all joy, my brothers, when you meet trials of various kinds, ESV

God's *purifying discipline* will *begin* with the house of God. God desires that His followers walk in holiness, and for most of us, that might require some painful circumstances before we fully submit to the will of God in our self-directed, busy, distracted, earth-focused lives.

1 Peter 4:17 For the time is come that judgment must begin at the house of God: and if it first begin at <u>us</u>, what shall the end be of them that obey not the gospel of God? ESV

Through painful circumstances, God's people will mature and draw nearer to him. Complacent believers will abandon their self-rule and finally allow God to *fully* use them to witness and set an example for the rest of the world, the earth-dwellers. *Imposters,* however, will abandon the "front-lines" and run to the world for temporal comfort. They'll abandon the *ultimate* reward of their salvation, eternal life, for the deceitful promises of avoiding rejection and discomfort by cozying up to the world.

So many believers will be disillusioned with God when greater trials and tribulation really start ramping up and they still have their feet on the ground. Their symbolic "lamps" will not be full of "oil" to get through the entire symbolic "night" because they never believed they had to wait for the bridegroom who would be coming *after* great peril and tribulation. Some will abandon the faith because they believed a *false* report, and counted on an *early rescue*. In the parable of the ten virgins, the bridegroom was delayed, according to the expectations of the foolish. But actually, he's right on time.

I suggest that we start acquiring the necessary "oil" right now. Belief comes by reading, meditating on, and obeying God's holy Word. Your "oily faith" will be evident to you and others when your *daily* life reflects your focused intention and preparation as God's end-times witness to the lost and dying world.

> **Matthew 25:1-13** Then shall the kingdom of heaven be likened unto ten virgins, which took their lamps, and went forth to meet the bridegroom. And five of them were wise, and five were foolish. They that were foolish took their lamps, and took no oil with them: But the wise took oil in their vessels with their lamps. While the bridegroom tarried, they all slumbered and slept. And at midnight there was a cry made, Behold, the bridegroom cometh; go ye out to meet him. Then all those virgins arose, and trimmed their lamps. And the foolish said unto the wise, Give us of your oil; for our lamps are gone out. But the wise answered, saying, Not so; lest there be not enough for us and you: but go ye rather to them that sell, and buy for yourselves. And while they went to buy, the bridegroom came; and they that were ready went in with him to the marriage: and the door was shut. Afterward came also the other virgins, saying, Lord, Lord, open to us. But he answered and said, Verily I say unto you, I know you not. Watch therefore, for ye know neither the day nor the hour wherein the Son of man cometh.

That Day may not be comfortable reading for many believers because some of the perspectives presented will contradict what Christians have been taught for the last several decades. With all due diligence, however, the content will *not* contradict Scripture. I hope that a careful reading of this book leaves all genuine truth-seekers with new insights concerning the chronology of the time and events of the tribulation. This book attempts an honest examination of the authenticity of a pretribulation rapture, and will take the reader through the twenty-two chapters of Revelation, with commentary, in order to examine biblical prophecy with deeper insights.

Read *That Day* entirely, and try to digest every word of it. Hopefully, you will have your spiritual eyes opened to astonishing biblical truth. If you have never considered the *historical* position of the Church, that Christ will return *after* the Church suffers persecution and tribulation under the governance and direction of the Antichrist, you *will* encounter that prophetic viewpoint here.

I do not assume to be 100 percent right about every perspective I hold, but I am convinced that I did adequate research and fervently sought the Lord's guidance for this prophetic interpretation of Revelation. My prayer is that every reader will take seriously what the Word of God says, especially in Revelation, the summation of all biblical prophecy.

I continue to study the amazing book of Revelation and find more rich nuggets of truth each time. Revelation is the book of God's final appeal to mankind, and everyone should consider carefully what God has declared.

If in the end, you and I differ in theological positions about eschatology, I only ask that you choose your position based on the *clear* words of God in scripture, and not based on the popular teachings of so many honorable pastors, teachers, and authors, even the majority of Christians, who seemingly march to the same rhythm, with *conjectural* viewpoints for their theological positions. Investigate the Word of God yourself. Don't just follow the "Pied Piper".

One's eschatological beliefs are not considered an essential of the faith, so we all must exercise love, peace, and gentleness, without discord, toward those whose prophetic appraisals differ from our own. Even with differences in our private prophetic positions, Christians must continue to strive together to be about God's business, enlarging *His* kingdom, rescuing lost sinners, loving the brethren, and loving one another, as God loves us. *We* are the characters in God's story, in the *last* chapter of His holy Scriptures.

Table of Contents

PART ONE

Index of Terms

The Index of Terms is presented to assist the reader in understanding the biblical meaning of prophetic terms used in in this book, and in the book of Revelation, based on a preponderance of scriptural evidence. Unless otherwise noted, scriptural references used in the book will come from the King James Bible.

The saints are not deceased humans, canonized by earthly churches. They are the *spiritual* Church, those who have been born again to new life in Christ. The saints are *the redeemed*. In the book of Revelation, they are those who suffer under the Antichrist in the tribulation. The saints are a metaphorical heavenly New Jerusalem. Peter, in 1 Peter 2:5, says that the redeemed are a spiritual house and a holy priesthood. *All* believers are saints. There is not a separate or select group of saints, based on ethnicity or good deeds. The saints are also referred to as *the house of God*.

> **Ephesians 2:17-22** And he came and preached peace to you who were far off and peace to those who were near. For through him we *both* have access in one Spirit to the Father.

> So then you are no longer strangers and aliens, but you are fellow citizens *with the saints* and members of the household of God, built on the foundation of the *apostles and prophets*, Christ Jesus himself being the cornerstone, in whom *the whole structure, being joined together*, grows into a holy temple in the Lord. In him you also are being built *together* into a dwelling place for God by the Spirit. ESV

Salvation is a gift from God that cannot be earned by good works, but only through repentance of sin and receiving Jesus Christ as Savior and Lord. The reward of this gift is eternal life.

Earth-dweller is a term shortened from phrases that describe the lost as: "they that dwell upon the earth," (Rev. 11:10) "the inhabiters of the earth" (Rev. 8:13; 12:12) and "the dwellers on earth whose names have *not* been written in the book of life from the foundation of the world" (Rev. 17:8). These are wicked, unrighteous rebels who dwell on the earth. They have no love for God, and they despise the Church as well. The dwellers on earth are referred to frequently throughout Revelation. The earth-dwellers are sometimes referred to as "*the world.*"

Gog and Magog is a representation of every nation on earth, who by policy and action, tries to eliminate the witness of the saints, and cast away the presence of God. Gog and Magog depict the *earth-dwellers* (wicked people) in battle against God in the battle of Armageddon at the end of time.

Armageddon Satan and his evil forces have been waging war against God and his saints throughout the history of the world. (for a "thousand years") At the end of the world (the end of the symbolic millennium,) Satan will be loosed by God, to rise up in a final cataclysmic war against God, to challenge God for rights to God's kingdom. Just prior to this war, the rapture of the Church occurs. The war of Armageddon will *quickly* be over-ruled by God, and terminated. (Rev. 16:16–17.) The last vial of God's wrath is poured out on the people of the earth, and then God loudly proclaims, "It is done."

The actual short-lived final battle of Armageddon is described in Revelation 19:19–21, although it occurs at the end of the seal and trumpet judgments of God, on the symbolic "*last* day." This is the same battle described by Ezekiel in Ezekiel 38 and 39. The *Gog-Magog* Battle is also Armageddon.

The Millennium is a figurative period of the amount of time that God works in the earth to completely redeem mankind and destroy evil forever. The millennium is a *figurative* 1,000 years, or a long, perfect amount of time. The millennium started with the church age and will end at the second coming of Christ. At the end of the millennium, just before the return of Christ, God's current *restraint* on Satan's power and freedom of action will be *lifted*. Satan will make war against the saints, and over-come them, but only temporarily, and by *God's* decree.

At the end, just prior to the second coming, the devil will be *loosed* out of his prison, the abyss, the place where he operates now. He is currently *bound* by God and *cannot* have *full* reign. God's firm security over Satan ensures that he will not operate in such a way as to deceive whole nations. He *cannot* overcome a man's freewill. He *can*, however, deceive, accuse, and tempt, and bring harm and evil into the earth, but he does *not* have the power of death. He does *not* have power over the Church. Satan is cast out of heaven and "*bound*" but still has a great degree of destructive powers *allowed by God* until the day of wrath. *To believe that Satan is bound* does *not* necessitate a belief that Satan's influence is *absent* in the world.

Seven represents *complete, whole, universal,* or *perfect* in apocalyptic language. What comes in sevens in Revelation emanates from God. There are dozens of references to the *symbolic number* seven in the book of Revelation. There are seven candlesticks, stars, letters, Spirits, seals, trumpets, thunders, heads, angels, bowls, mountains, blessings, and so forth.

Seven years is symbolic of a complete and perfect number of years for God to complete his redemption plan on earth.

Thousand is a symbolic number, that typically means *immensity, fullness of quantity, timeless, or multitude.* Thousand evokes a very large number or an extended period of time, according to most Bible passages. There are numerous examples of the number thousand, being figurative of a large number throughout the scriptures. Below are examples of *thousand* being figurative of a large number, not an exact number.

> **Psalm 50:10** For every beast of the forest is mine, and the cattle upon *a thousand hills.*

> **Deut. 1:11** The Lord God of your fathers make you a *thousand* times so many more as ye are, and bless you, as he hath promised you.

> **Deut. 7:9** Know therefore that the Lord thy God, he is God, the faithful God, which keepeth covenant and mercy with

them that love him and keep his commandments to a *thousand generations*

Deut. 32:30 How should one chase a *thousand*, and two put ten *thousand* to flight, except their Rock had sold them, and the Lord had shut them up?

Joshua 23:10 One man of you shall chase a *thousand*: for the Lord your God, he it is that fighteth for you, as he hath promised you.

1 Samuel 18:13 Therefore Saul removed him from him, and made him his captain over a *thousand*; and he went out and came in before the people.

Job 33:23 If there be a messenger with him, an interpreter, one among a *thousand*, to shew unto man his uprightness:

Psalm 84:10 For a day in thy courts is better than a *thousand*. I had rather be a doorkeeper in the house of my God, than to dwell in the tents of wickedness.

Psalm 91:7 For a *thousand* years in thy sight are but as yesterday when it is past, and as a watch in the night.

Psalm 105:8 He hath remembered his covenant forever, the word which he commanded to a *thousand* generations.

Isaiah 7:23 And it shall come to pass in that day, that every place shall be, where there were a *thousand* vines at a *thousand* silverlings, it shall even be for briers and thorns.

Isaiah 30:17 One *thousand* shall flee at the rebuke of one; at the rebuke of five shall ye flee: till ye be left as a beacon upon the top of a mountain, and as an ensign on an hill.

Isaiah 60:22 A little one shall become a *thousand*, and a small one a strong nation: I the Lord will hasten it in his time.

2 Peter 3:8 But, beloved, be not ignorant of this one thing, that one day is with the Lord as a *thousand* years, and a *thousand* years as one day.

Judges 15:15–16, Jeremiah 32:18, Genesis 20:16, Song of Solomon 4:4, Amos 5:3, Jude 1:14

Three and a half days is a symbolic number for a brief period of time.

The Church, prior to the advent of Jesus Christ, includes all God's followers and worshipful believers who called upon the name of the Lord in faith. (Gen. 4:26) The people who lived *before* Jesus came to earth, looked *forward* to a coming Messiah. Today, believers look *back* to the Messiah who *came.* All who genuinely call on Jesus Christ for his grace, to forgive them and save them from their personal sin, make up the "Church." Both the Old Testament and New Testament Church exercise faith in the *same* Savior, Jesus Christ.

Hebrews 11:13–16 These all died in faith, *(Moses, Enoch, Abraham, Sarah, Noah, Isaac, Jacob, Joseph …)* not having received the promises, but having seen them afar off, and were persuaded of them, and embraced them, and confessed that they were strangers and pilgrims on the earth. For they that say such things declare plainly that they seek a country. And truly, if they had been mindful of that country from whence they came out, they might have had opportunity to have returned. But now they desire a better country, that is, an heavenly: wherefore *God is not ashamed to be called their God*: for he hath prepared for them a city.

The Church is *one* body of believers. There is *no* partition between those who are in Christ, whether Jew or Gentile. Christ made *one* new man of the two groups.

Note: I capitalize the word *Church* when referring to *the spiritual Church*, and not to a brick and mortar building or religious institution.

> **Ephesians 2:13-16** *But now* in Christ Jesus you who once were far off have been brought near by the blood of Christ. For he himself is our peace, who has made us both *one* and has broken down in his flesh the dividing wall of hostility by abolishing the law of commandments expressed in ordinances, that he might create in himself *one new man* in place of the two, so making peace, and might reconcile us both to God *in one body* through the cross, thereby killing the hostility. ESV

The 144,000 in the book of Revelation are *all* of God's witnesses on earth, both redeemed Jews and Gentiles alike. Revelation 7:9 increases this number by a *literal* interpretation, where John actually *sees* a great multitude "which no man could number" and which includes the whole company of the redeemed.

This number, 144,000, is symbolic of the twelve *tribes* who represent the redeemed *Jews, and* the twelve *apostles* who represent the redeemed *Gentiles.* The number twelve, in apocalyptic language represents a *complete* and *perfect* number. The number *1,000* is typically symbolic of a multitude, or very large number. (12 ×12 × 1,000) or 12 × 12 × the multitude. 12 × 12 × 1,000 = 144,000) This is symbolic of the *complete Church*, from every age.

> **Ephesians 2:19** So then you are no longer strangers and aliens, but you are fellow citizens with the saints and members of the household of God, built on *the foundation of the apostles and prophets,* Christ Jesus himself being the cornerstone, ESV

Moses and Elijah were God's appointed witnesses in the Old Testament times. They were the mouthpieces of God, and had power to bring affliction to the earth. In the New Testament book of Revelation, *these two men are metaphorical for God's "two" end-time witnesses in the earth,* which are *all* the representatives of the elect Church of God on earth, inclusive of both born-again Jews and Gentiles. They are *not* two literal men in the book of Revelation. They *represent* the whole company of faithful witnesses on earth.

Moses and Elijah were with Jesus at his transfiguration (Mark 9:4–7). Moses represented the *Law* and Elijah the *Prophets.* God spoke to these two mean and told them to *listen to Jesus.* This was God instructing mankind that the Law and the Prophets must now yield to Jesus. Jesus is the *completion* of the Law, and the *fulfillment* of all that Moses and the prophets spoke. Jesus is the only way into the presence of God.

God gave Moses the Law, and Elijah was a prophet who proclaimed a coming judgment if the people did not repent of their sin and idolatry. God's *end-time witnesses*, like Moses and Elijah, will also prophesy of God's coming judgments on the wicked if there is no repentance. It is *not* going to be a painless task. Witnesses generally *suffer* as a result of bringing this unpopular message to rebellious people. In the very end, thankfully, God's witnesses *will* be vindicated, just as Moses and Elijah were. It will be glorious.

Two-Witnesses are *all* of the representatives of the elect Church of God on earth, inclusive of both born-again *Jews and Gentiles*. (Called *Moses and Elijah* in Revelation 11.) Revelation 11:4 says they are *the two candlesticks* and the *two olive trees* standing before the God of the earth. They are killed in Revelation 11:7. After a short time (a symbolic 3 ½ days) they hear God's great voice saying, "Come up hither." The Church, all of God's faithful witnesses, rise up to be with the Lord in the air, on the great and glorious day of the rapture.

> *"The two olive trees," which supply the material for the candlesticks, are fit emblems of the Old and New Testaments; the candlesticks typify the Jewish and Christian Churches. These are identical so far as being God's witnesses; the Church derives her stores from the Word of God, the light of the Word of God is manifested through the Church."* [1]

Jerusalem and the Temple are figurative of the *true believers*, the faithful followers of Jesus Christ.

The First Resurrection is when believers' souls awake from the dead and are transported to Paradise. At the *end* of the symbolic thousand year millennium, which is also the end of the symbolic *seven* year tribulation period, all saints of every age will meet the Lord in the air to reign with Christ eternally. Jesus taught that the dead in Christ *immediately* go to Paradise, which is the intermediate heaven (Luke 23:43). Every believer takes part in the *first resurrection*, upon their death, throughout this entire millennium. The *first resurrection* is culminated at the rapture of the Church.

From their resting place in Paradise, these saints await the end of Tribulation "first resurrection," when they will meet with the living saints, and *all* get their glorified bodies. God will bring *all* His saints together, to join Him in the air as He descends to earth for a spectacular day of vindication of his family. All the people of God, of every age, will accompany Jesus and all His angels and armies to a battle where He will finally and completely destroy the Man of Sin, and conquer evil forever.

The Intermediate Heaven is a place where believers and unbelievers go when they die, to wait for their bodily resurrection. Scripture teaches that we are eternal beings, so when we die, we go somewhere else to live. The intermediate heaven for faithful *believers* is also called *Paradise*. The saved go to Paradise, or *Heaven*, to await glorified bodies, and *the unsaved go to Hades* to await judgment.

Jesus is in this intermediate heaven ruling and reigning with all those who have died, trusting in him alone for redemption. While on earth, before he was sentenced to die, Jesus told Pilate that he had a kingdom, but it was not of this world. He also told his followers to pray that his kingdom would come. He concluded his written testament, with an admonition for the bride of Christ to say, "Come."

> **Revelation 21:2** And I John saw the holy **city**, new Jerusalem, coming down from God out of heaven, prepared as a bride adorned for her husband.

This city-bride is the Church. What we have here is a picture of *all* the saints of God in the intermediate heaven, descending with God, to meet the rest of the body of Christ in the air.

Three and a half years is a symbolic period of time for *half of seven years*—a symbolic perfect number. This uncertain, but limited, space of time since the creation of the world, symbolizes the time during which the Church is to suffer oppression. Three and a half years is also called twelve hundred and sixty days; a time, and times, and half a time; a time and times and the dividing of time; and forty-two months in prophetic scripture.

The Rapture is a biblical belief that the faithful, living followers of Jesus Christ will be removed from the earth to heaven, in concert with all the dead *saints*, to meet Jesus Christ in the air. The rapture is a rescue of God's people from among the wicked on earth. It will happen *prior* to God's final judgments. First Thessalonians 4:13–17 depicts this coming of Christ to rescue his people as a *loud*, spectacular, and *visible* event. A loud *trumpet of God* (*not* a Christian dog whistle that only Christians can hear) will be blown by a mighty angel. There will be loud *shouts* and *voices* coming from the host of heaven and the archangel of God. *Thunderings* and *lightening*, as well as a *massive earthquake*, all pretty much point to *the loudest event in scripture.* God's own voice booms, "*Come up hither.*" (Rev. 11:12). And all the saints, of all time, meet the Lord in the air.

A day in prophetic writing, is symbolic of *a short amount of time* and does not limit its meaning to twenty-four hours. God operates outside of time and space. In prophetic writing, "day" is also the figurative amount of time that God will use in His vindication and *final* rescue of His chosen people. On the last *day*, often called "*that day*," God will destroy his enemies in a final battle, and put down evil, eternally. (God can accomplish a figurative thousand years' worth of work in a short "day" of time.) God does not need to rely on man's calendars and clocks to accomplish anything.

> **2 Peter 3:8** But, beloved, do not forget this one thing, that with the Lord one day is as a thousand years, and a thousand years as one day.

Priests The priesthood of God is the birthright of every born-again believer. Christians are a holy nation to God—a royal priesthood, with direct access to God (1 Pet. 2:9; Heb. 4:16). All faithful believers are God's representatives on Earth, and have the responsibility of communicating what God has said in His Word to the world.

CHAPTER I

A Prophetic Message to the Church

I had an unusual and epic dream after a long, summer day of motorcycle riding along the Atlantic coast with my husband. This dream haunted me for several days because it was so vivid. I believe God wanted me to learn something from it. I also think it has a timely message for the body of Christ. After nearly seven hours of riding, just before a misty, lonely darkness enveloped us, my husband and I came upon a remote ocean-view hotel along our unfamiliar coastal route. Weary and exhausted, we checked in, and then climbed the outside stairwell to our room. Soon, we were settled into a comfy, warm bed for some well-needed rest. Sleep, beautiful sleep, was on the way.

I surely did sleep, but I dreamed like never before. I don't know what made me dream so vividly that night, but what a vivid dream I had. It was so vivid and epic that I felt it could possibly be a God-sent dream. It was in technicolor—a real "big-screen" kind of dream, full of details that were still available to my memory when I awoke. When fully awake, I asked God what the dream could be telling me. A Bible verse immediately impressed me as to its meaning. At the time, I could not exactly quote it, but I knew what the verse basically said. I looked it up. This is the Bible verse from 1 Peter 4:18: *"And if the righteous scarcely be saved, where shall the ungodly and the sinner appear?"* Now for the dream.

The setting for my dream started at a small hotel along a remote ocean road—just like where we were staying. In this dream, I woke up in the middle of the night, really thirsty. I decided to get up and go find some water, as we apparently had none in our room. (I know. Dreams are strange.) I was in skimpy sleepwear, but I walked right out of our room without any hesitation down the hall to the ice machine. There was no ice, so I just kept going. Barefoot, I walked downstairs and right outside into the parking lot. Not a soul was in sight. A quiet, salty, haze swirled through the air. I saw both of our bikes in the lot, but our car was there as well. Strange. I got into our car and drove off, in search of somewhere to buy drinking water.

The coastal street I navigated, and every street I looked down, was dreadfully deserted. Dim neon lights, lit-up patches in the distance, were far away from the crashing waves off to my left. I slowly drove along, wondering what was I thinking to be out here on the streets all alone?

Finally, I saw a small gathering of people out on the beach side of the street. Slowing the car, I yelled to them, "Hey, where can I buy some water around here?" Just as a girl who appeared to be the center of attention started to speak, a monstrous wave roared over them all, pulling them into the ocean depths, claiming every one of them. It just swept them away into the pitch darkness of the sea, right in front of my eyes. I paused, wide-eyed and mouth hanging open. Horrified, I quickly rolled up the window and sped further down the unfamiliar road. I thought I had better turn the car around on a side street, and head back to the hotel. The road was curving away from the beach. The next side street I came to was a short street on the beachside.

At the end of this quaint street, I was attracted to a small wooden house with a dim light on inside. I pulled up, got out of the car, and knocked on the door. An elderly woman with haunted eyes answered the door and hastily invited me inside. As I crossed her dimly lit room toward the back of the house, I was immediately focused on her massive picture window being pummeled by enormous waves. I observed her frail hands trembling, and watched her scared, brown eyes ready to spill a flood of tears. I sensed that she wanted to fall into my arms for hope and reassurance that everything was going to be okay. She wanted to be rescued. I stiffened, not wanting to be involved with the complications of her rescue.

Here I was standing in a little old lady's front room in my scant sleepwear, which was never meant to be worn out in public. What was I doing? I left my resting place with careless haste, and now I felt unprotected myself. I had just witnessed several people out on the street getting swept away by the very same monster that was knocking on this lady's picture window. My husband didn't even know I was missing. I suddenly felt that my mission to find some special drinking water was foolish and vain. There certainly was drinking water somewhere at our hotel, but I went looking for better water. I was too self-focused, independent, and careless. Now I just wanted to find my way back to the safety of our hotel. The thirst that called me was no longer there.

In this dream, I knew that I was a child of God and that I, personally, was safe in Christ, but nevertheless I sensed that cataclysmic judgment was imminent. I had an awareness that I should help this lady, but I also knew that I must get back where I was supposed to be. Everything around me was ready to be crushed and claimed by the darkness and the deep. I wished I didn't go out alone. I was too hasty and independent, and now I needed my family—my spouse. Together, we would not have simply run back to safety, and there would have been a different ending. We each have different strengths and talents, and combined, a bit more wisdom too. Doing things the wrong way sometimes leaves regrets.

I am going to cut out details to get to the finish. I left this feeble and defenseless little old lady there all alone, in a place of imminent danger. I drove back to the hotel on the same road, which was now a littered, wet, and sloppy trail, covered with sand and debris. I parked our car in the hotel parking lot and ran up the staircase to the dark, quiet, cozy room. I crept inside, got back into bed, and went back to sleep. End of dream. Weird, huh?

Ponder some of the messages that could be in this dream. Most of the people in this dream *suddenly* went into eternity. One blink and they were all gone. The part that really unsettled me is that *I* was a careless woman in this dream. I abandoned good sense to recklessly pursue a drink of water. (In the end, I found out I wasn't even really thirsty.) I went out without a "covering." I consulted *no one* when I ventured out into the world and was *unprepared* for danger. I couldn't help anyone because I was vulnerable and disconnected.

I wish that the dream showed me reaching out to help the elderly lady instead of just driving away and going back to bed. Why didn't I do more to rescue this frightened woman? Why were my garments so thoughtless and unacceptable when I went into the world on my little mission? That was my own improper choice. Maybe my skimpy garments represent God's people going out into the world without a necessary prayer covering.

Well, the dream ended with me safely back to my hotel room. God is faithful to his own, even when we aren't. He brings us back. He guides and directs his children. We might make wrong turns along the way, and attempt to be independent, but we need to lean on the Master in *every* situation. We need to always be about God's business, whether on the main road or on a seemingly God-forsaken, off-the-beaten path, sloppy, soggy trail of a road. We can't just lay our head down in comfort and forget about those needy souls all around us. We have work to do for the Master's kingdom.

Our express mission in this world is to be productive in serving God. We need to live for His glory and expand His kingdom, *wherever He leads us.* Our hearts need to be moved with compassion for all the weary sheep without a shepherd. We need to attempt to help the soul-sick, empty, and frightened people whenever we are privileged to have some "door" to walk through into their lives. Every encounter that God gives us with the lost is a *spiritual* opportunity. Our Great Commission from God is: "Go ye therefore, and teach all nations, baptizing them in the name of the Father, and of the Son, and of the Holy Ghost: Teaching them to observe all things whatsoever I have commanded you" (Matt. 28:19–20).

So let's *go* into the world, as soldiers into battle. Let's plunder the devil's illegitimate kingdom. Let's expect to win souls, being careful to select all the right armor. We know that we have an awesome and powerful Commander who goes before and behind us. We have everything to gain by just being obedient. Let's gather the lost, wherever we are able. So now what?

"All right." you say. "I'm ready to go to battle for the Lord. I'm ready to face the enemy and plunder hell." It may sound like a simple proclamation, but this might be how it really plays out. "Hey, where are you, God? I'm out here without much backup. Things are getting rough down here on earth. Hello. Are you there? Reporting for duty, Lord."

"Hey, God, innocent children died today. Our law-enforcement families are losing daddies to senseless violence. Hundreds of babies are being intentionally ripped from the safety of their mother's wombs. Do you even care? Are you our Commander in Chief? My family doesn't feel safe. Do you see all the rioting and looting going on? Do you see the racial tension, poverty, injustices, and drug addictions?

"Hey, God, we're starting to lose our confidence. Look what they are doing to our president and his family. Lies and deception appear to be winning. Why is this happening? There's a plague of violence in our cities, and we have a pandemic going on. Are you there, God? The body count is rising. People are afraid. The Church is starting to doubt. We are looking up and waiting to escape this turmoil and tribulation. When are you going to rescue us? Where are you?"

And then discouragement comes.

Is God really with us? The prophetic book of Revelation is the book with answers. We will see in this book that God most certainly *is* with us, and He really *is* going to rescue His people. As a matter of fact, He will accomplish much more than our rescue. He will fulfil *all* things written in the entire Bible. Not one prophecy will go unfulfilled. (That means some unprecedented days lie ahead of us.) Both the Church, (as defined in the *terms*) and all unbelievers are the characters in the dramatic events of Revelation. *We* are in this last book of the Bible, so it is imperative for us to know what it says and what it means for *us*. Could we soon be living in these bizarre last days of time, as described in Revelation?

John, a close friend and disciple of Jesus, is recognized as the author of Revelation. He wrote Revelation in his early nineties, on a remote Asian island named Patmos. John was banished to this prison island for his testimony of Jesus Christ. While on this island, the Holy Spirit told him to write a revelation of Jesus Christ as King of kings and Lord of lords. John was instructed to *unveil*, or reveal, *Jesus Christ* as *one God, with the Father,* and as the *Alpha and Omega, the Creator and Redeemer.* Revelation comes from the Greek word *apokalypsis,* which means "unveiling." That is why Revelation is also called the *Apocalypse.*

John was also called by God to write about events that will happen during *the last days on earth* before the second coming of Christ. His writing was not meant to produce a chronological *story.* It was meant to encourage the Church to remain *faithful* to God and trust God's plan. The *Holy Spirit* told John to write what he *saw* in visions, not explain what he saw, just simply write it (Rev. 1:11,19; 21:5.)

God *demonstrated* the contents of Revelation to John *through signs and symbols* (Rev. 1:1; 10:4). Divine truth was imparted to John through *visions,* which contained some rather unusual and distressing *signs* and *symbols*. Revelation is organized by the *timing* of John's visions, making his presentation of events *recursive* and non-chronological. John writes about nightmarish events and then moves on to others. He then goes back to *previous* events and adds different and additional details to produce more insights and add information. When reading Revelation, we must completely set aside our *bias* of a sequential and chronological timeline, as relating to John's visions. His visions are *not* sequential and chronological.

According to John's inspired writings, *everyone* should read, observe, and obey the teachings of Revelation. There are promised blessings for doing so (Rev. 1:3). It is not sufficient nor beneficial to just simply breeze through the words of Revelation thoughtlessly. Our goal is to arrive at the *truth* by examining the scriptures carefully. To do this, we will have to read Revelation without bringing presuppositions into our study. Simply consider what the written Word of God says, not what other authors, movies, and teachers have taught us.

The holy Bible is the sole authority about end-times matters, not *my* perspective. I have only aimed to line up my perspective with what God's written Word actually says. Should I miss the mark in any interpretation or conclusion, stick with the Word of God. I don't claim to have it all figured out, nor am I infallible. My hope is that this book encourages readers to study this most important and final book of the Bible, Revelation, and in so doing, be blessed by God.

I hope that in this study, believers are encouraged to always maintain *an eternal perspective* and keep the faith. We need to remember that God has already won the victory, is winning now (even if things are looking bad), and that God *will* have a great and glorious, victorious vindication, and spectacular win in the end. What is happening on earth today is all a part of God's divine and decreed plan.

Christians of *every* age, and in *this* day, must remain faithful to God, even among the unholy, unrighteous, enemies of God. God's enemies are mounting up. Who can't see that? Satan is attempting to build his own kingdom on earth, devoid of God. He's making the nations ready for his *final showdown against God* in an attempt to *usurp* God. We, the Church, are in *this* end-time Revelation story. It is not *someone else* who must remain faithful to God in the tumultuous times ahead, it is *you and me.*

Like John, *we* will also see strange unimaginable sights in the future. We will see significant changes in the world and unparalleled shocking events taking place. America and the rest of the world will not remain as they have been in our lifetimes because mankind is *rapidly* losing their fear of God. Of course, typical change is always taking place, but peace will soon be taken from *the earth*, both politically and economically. Spiritual darkness and demonic deception will envelop the earth like a heavy veil. This won't be the typical antics of Satan; it will be *God's* judgment. While this *judgment* is for *unrighteous* rebels, and *not* the *faithful* followers of Jesus Christ, scripture is clear that *the saints* will be here, nonetheless, and will be affected by the climate of God's judgment on sinners.

When John records an event, our bias would assume that the next event he records *follows* that event, as it would on a chronological timeline. But John's writing is *recursive, not sequential*. Because we relate to the passing of time horizontally and chronologically, we naturally read John's writings with this *bias*. Who would ever know that our concept of sequential time is a *bias*. The events happening in Revelation are more *accurately* arranged *vertically*, and often *simultaneously*, more like a hailstorm, coming *down* from God. Picture *falling judgments*, not a timeline of events.

Besides writing *vertically*, John wrote symbolically with biblical *allegory*. Typically readers of Revelation want to know what all the signs and symbols *mean*. We might try to make the symbols *literal*, but Revelation is *not* a literal book. The characters and numbers are *symbolic*. It is not necessary that we understand every sign or symbol in the book of Revelation, *as if it were possible,* to completely solve this book as a mystery puzzle. If we dwell on the *meaning* of every symbol, we will miss the *spiritual message*. One of the worst misfortunes of reading Revelation with the intent of turning allegorical symbols into modern-day, specific, literal characters and events, is that *the main message really is spiritual.* We get hung up on the wrong things in this book.

We cannot put a *literal* interpretation on all the visions that John had centuries ago. Remember, the Holy Spirit didn't dictate twenty-first-century *words* to John. He could have. God simply told him to write what he *saw*. God gave John the *visions*, not the *words*. John saw *unimaginable* symbolic characters and events, in very *modern* environments over 2,000 years down the road. They probably shook him to his core. He had to *describe* these characters and scenes from his limited human perspective, so he used *similes*, such as *like* and *as*, preceding unusual descriptions. No one in John's day had ever seen such things before. (e.g., "their power is in their mouths and in their tails: for their tails were like unto serpents and had heads," and "horse-shaped locusts with crowns of gold and faces of men.") Bizarre sights.

As Christians, *we* are *the called*. Today, we, the called are God's own chosen *witnesses*, in such a time as this. *We* are *chosen* to be *faithful* followers of Jesus Christ, even to our own peril and death, right now in *this* day and time. Few of us have ever faced any serious peril or threat for being God's ambassadors, but the chances are growing that we soon will. John's visions are unfolding in *our* lifetime. *We* will see *down-spiraling changes* in morals, governments, economic stability, and human suffering. *We* will be mocked, humiliated, and despised by the world, including by some of our loved ones. Do not fear. This scenario is *God-decreed*. God will never abandon us.

The book of Revelation *ends* well for all the faithful saints of God. Let that sink in. Jesus showed John how He will gloriously rescue us *at His second coming*. This is the blessed hope of the Church. But most of us want to know if it will it happen *before* we experience any real pain and suffering on the earth. Let's see. There just happens to be one exceptional and legitimate clue as to *when* our rescue comes. Here is *a major clue* about the *timing* of our rescue. *The dead in Christ will rise* from their graves to meet the Lord in the air *at the same moment in time* as the rapture of living saints. So *when* do the dead in Christ rise from their graves? I'm glad you asked. We will find out in this study.

When John reports his vision of the *last day rescue* in Revelation 6 and 11, *that* is the rapture, but it is *not* the end of the Revelation. (Hint: I just told you the answer to your "When?" question.) Revelation 6 and 11 depict simultaneous judgments coming from God on the *symbolic last day* at the end of time. But John has a lot more to *communicate* from God. *After* reporting that the *last* trumpet sounds and the witnesses are *rescued*, we then see the sky roll up, the stars fall, and a huge earthquake shake the mountains flat. What more could John report as happening on earth? *It's over!* To *continue* reporting, John will *flashback* to earlier judgments that he previously reported, to fill in some important gaps.

Revelation is God's last prophetic message to the Church. This final book of the Bible informs that at the *end* of the world, God will gather his own children from among his enemies. Immediately *following* this rescue, God's final judgment will be delivered worldwide in a final battle, as Satan rises up with all the earth-dwellers to oppose God's authority. (Review the definition of *earth-dweller* in the terms section.) God will destroy every one of these foolish, wicked, and unrighteous rebels who despise his coming. He will conquer evil and death in *that day*. The whole earth and all the celestial bodies will be burned up and dissolved in a fiery blaze in *that day*. Satan will be cast alive into hell, the lake of fire and brimstone. God will then create a new heaven and new earth for His people.

You might be saying, "Wait a minute. I don't like this version of the last days. I was taught that Christians will fly away when Satan's intense opposition and persecutions start to come against the Church. I was taught that we'll all be dining up in heaven with Jesus at a well-set table of delicacies during the time of hideous suffering on earth. Jesus is only supposed to purge, purify, and redeem *His Jewish family* during the tribulation. *Christians* are supposed to be transported to heaven *before* the second coming. Why should *we* pay a price to be counted worthy of our calling?"

Many Christians believe this way. They typically defend their belief with the words and teachings of popular and progressive pastors, prophecy ministries, books, family, friends, and movies. These mistaken sources have been informing the Church for the last few decades, what they think we should believe about the *timing* of the rapture. The problem with their pretribulation rapture theory, however, is that it does *not* align itself with the *clear* words of scripture.

Those who are waiting for a pretribulation secret rapture are *not* waiting for the second coming of Christ by their own admission. Pretribulation believers claim that the rapture is *not* a "*coming.*" But didn't Jesus admonish believers to be ready for His *coming?* He even informed that it's *not* going to happen when people suspect it is.

> **Matthew 24:44** Therefore be ye also ready: for in such an hour as ye think *not* the Son of man cometh.

Those who hold fast to *pretribulation* teaching are ready for a silent and secret call from Jesus to join him in the air at any moment. They anticipate being suddenly raptured *before* the Antichrist is revealed, adorned like a bride, and pampered with a sumptuous wedding feast, while all hell is breaking loose on the earth. They see themselves as being Christ's favored bride and avoiding all serious suffering for their testimony in the tribulation period. Believe me, I understand that no one wants to suffer, but scripture indicates clearly that universal suffering is going to happen on earth *prior* to the rapture. The Church is not excluded.

The *faithful* are going to suffer. This is nothing new. All uncompromising Christ-followers have suffered persecution in every age since the beginning of creation—some more than others. Consider that missionaries and others, world-wide, are being seriously persecuted and even tortured *today*. Christians in foreign lands have limbs chopped off and their homes burned down *today*. Christians in the workplace are silenced by policy or shunned and mocked *today*.

> **2 Timothy 3:12** Indeed, *all* who desire to live a godly life in Christ Jesus *will* be persecuted.

Adherents to the *pre*tribulation rapture theory typically *do* believe that the rapture happens *in concert with the resurrection of the dead in Christ.* Together, all Christians will meet Jesus Christ in the air as He is descending toward the earth. This rescue, they believe, will happen prior to God's final judgment. Everything about those beliefs is *true*. So what's the problem?

The problem with a *pre*tribulation rapture is that it's *not biblical.* The Bible teaches that *the rapture will coincide with the day of the Lord. The day of the Lord is the second coming.* Nowhere in scripture does it teach that there is a silent, secret, halfway-to-earth, *not-second-coming, early-harvest* rapture of the Church *before* the tribulation. There is not a *second* seventh trumpet. God is no respecter of *Christians over Jews*, treating them to a banquet in heaven, while newly redeemed, born-again Jews are on earth being slaughtered and separated from the rest of their spiritual family. That is wrong theology.

Jesus Christ is coming back. He will return "as a thief" to those who are *not* watching and waiting for his return. His return for *them* will be *sudden* and *unannounced*. It will *not* be a stealth operation under the cover of darkness like the approach of a quiet, sneaky, prowling bandit. It will be *loud and spectacular*. The meaning of *"as a thief"* does not mean that Christ will *act like* a thief. Peter informs that this *"as a thief"* coming, will be *the day of the Lord* and will be *very noisy*.

> **2 Peter 3:10** But *the day of the Lord* will come *as a thief* in the night; in the which the heavens shall pass away *with a great noise*, and the elements shall melt with fervent heat, *the earth* also and the works that are therein *shall be burned up.*

There is *no* reason for the Church in this lukewarm and unholy generation to get an *escape pass* from the end-time trials and judgments that we read about in Revelation. Can you think of a scriptural reason why the last generation of people would not have to take up their cross daily and maneuver the "narrow road" *to the end?*

The professed believers in *our* day are no more special to God than any other generation of believers in history. Actually, many of the professing believers in the final generation on earth are deceived, lukewarm, and lovers of self, more than lovers of God. Many have re-created God in their imaginations to be more palatable to their taste. Of *all* the generations in history, it is doubtful that *this* compromised generation of professing, but nominal Christians would be God's favored bride, secretly called out of the world to escape the necessity of being an over-comer *to the end*. From *my* vantage point, *most* Christians today have much less time for God than their Prime, Netflix, and Firestick movies, along with their Facebook and social media surfing. They seek the "thumbs up" approval of social media friends over God's approval, based on the time given to each. Prayer and fasting today looks more like skipping a second dessert and asking God to bless everyone and everything (for five minutes between commercials or just before falling asleep at bedtime.) The Church is guilty and has strayed *far* from God.

The apostle Paul, in 2 Timothy 3:5, described the state of the Church in the last days. He said they do religious things, and appear as pious Christians to *others*, but they actually are *deceived* and don't really live the godly lives they appear to. Their flame for Christ is *low*. Their fire is *not* hot. They are *preoccupied* in the world. Yet hordes of these deceived and lukewarm Christians are waiting to be rescued, and they have "no flesh in the game."

> **2 Timothy 3:1–5** But understand this: In the last days terrible times will come. For men will be lovers of themselves, lovers of money, boastful, arrogant, abusive, disobedient to their parents, ungrateful, unholy, unloving, unforgiving, slanderous, without self-control, brutal, without love of good, traitorous, reckless, conceited, lovers of pleasure rather than lovers of God, *having a form of godliness but denying its power.* Turn away from such as these.

I know quite a number of people who think that because they believe *in* God and do a few good works for others, they will be going to heaven upon their death. I hope they do. But what

I have observed is that they do *not* glorify God as God. They don't really seek God, nor seek to *know* His Word. Romans 1 says that God will *not* tolerate and excuse men who hold the truth of God in unrighteousness. The Word says that it is the *wicked* who *knew* God, *but glorified him not as God.* That should put the fear of God in us.

> **Romans 1:21** Because that, *when they knew God, they glorified him not as God,* neither were thankful; but became vain in their imaginations, and their foolish heart was darkened.

Let's do our own personal appetite check. How much do we hunger for God? Do we spend time in His Word? Even the *devil* believes *in* God. That is *not* enough.

> **James 2:19** Thou believest that there is one God; thou doest well: the *devils* also believe, and tremble.

Our churches today are more focused on getting people to heaven than getting people *holy* and *ready* to meet God. "*Come to Jesus and get a heaven ticket. You will fly away with the Church in the rapture.*" People are joining churches for the *wrong reason,* a fire escape. They are not learning the importance of building a *relationship* with God and living in readiness and holiness. They do not understand the mission of the Church to work in the Master's harvest field. They do not understand that anything that robs our affection for God is an idol. They do not understand that all idols are demons.

Because the saints are *not* going to fly away *prior* to the tribulation judgments, the Church is being set up for a *huge* let-down and negative fallout when they become the object of hate and scorn worldwide. Our modern *miscalculation* of the timing of the rapture is primarily related to a lazy Church, *trusting popular voices* over the *clear* words of scripture.

Are *you* ready to *suffer* for Christ, or are you waiting for your white wedding apparel and a sumptuous meal in heaven to fill your belly with fabulous food in a carnal feast? Do you believe that the *last*-generation Christians hold a status with God above the saints of old, many whom were *martyred* for their faithfulness to Christ? What makes *this generation* so special that God would exempt *us* from the persecution that *every* one of his disciples endured? What makes us think that *we* are so special that God would choose to let *us* dine in heaven with Him, while a *different* second-coming harvest *of martyrs* is down on earth, being slaughtered? What *clear* scripture says that there will be *two* raptures and *two harvests*? Are we morally superior to those believers worldwide, who are *currently* languishing in confinement and tormented with persecution, simply because they follow Jesus Christ?

Okay, this is getting really uncomfortable. The time of tribulation has scary creatures, demonic malefactors, torment, war, and natural disasters like massive fires, pestilence, and famine. Are *we*, the Church, really supposed to see *ourselves* in this story, or is this only a book about what might happen to *someone else and definitely not to us*? Doesn't scripture say, 'But of that day and that hour knoweth no man, no, not the angels which are in heaven, *neither the Son*, but the Father' (Mark 13:32)?

Perhaps, in his *humanity*, Jesus did not know the day of His return, but that does *not* mean that God would never reveal the timing to the Son of God and the angels. *Jesus, in his deity, knows the day of his return.* Jesus is the one who opens the seven seals in Revelation, for heaven's sake. *He knows the time!* Even God's servants (the saints) are *not* in darkness as to knowing that the day of God's vengeance is very near.

> **1 Thessalonians 5:4** But *ye, brethren*, are *not* in darkness, that *that day* should overtake *you* as a thief.

> **Amos 3:7** Surely the Lord GOD will do nothing, but he revealeth his secret unto his servants the prophets.

It is *God* who chooses *when* mankind will understand the times, seasons, and spiritual symbols detailed in His Word. John certainly did not understand all of the prophecies that he wrote in Revelation. It was not for him to understand *at that time*. But that does not mean the mysteries of John's visions would forever remain mysterious. We understand a number of mysteries today that John was clueless about in the first century. God chooses to hide the meaning of *some* prophecies until the last days of time. In the book of Daniel, for instance, God said, "Go thy way, Daniel: for the words are closed up and sealed *till* the time of the *end*" (Dan. 12:9).

Prior to John's writing the book of Revelation, *Jesus* directly taught the people about the last days. Jesus was a master storyteller. He gave an analogy of the tumultuous last days by using physical symbolism in his teaching. Jesus used *analogy* in parables to communicate heavenly principles using earthly stories. One analogy Jesus used was of a woman in labor pains. The endtime judgments, Jesus said, would unfold like the contractions of a woman in labor. At first, he said, the pain would be mild and farther apart. As the time between contractions decreased, the pain of the contractions would grow intensely painful. So will it be with the end-time judgments.

Disastrous events and painful calamities are increasing at a pace like no other time in history. The distinction between truth and falsehood, right and wrong, righteousness and unrighteousness, is being made clear to *the true and faithful body of Christ*. Liars and deceivers are being exposed. However, *the spiritually blind masses* are now calling evil good and good evil. They *resist* the truth and cling to darkness and lies. Dividing lines are being drawn.

> **2 Thessalonians 10–12** And with all deceivableness of unrighteousness in them that perish; because they received not *the love of the truth*, that they might be saved. And *for this cause* God shall send them *strong* delusion, that they should believe a lie: That they all might be damned who believed not the truth, but had pleasure in unrighteousness.

We are fast approaching the most tumultuous times the world has ever known, the time known as the tribulation. (I refer to "tribulation" as the time *just prior to the second coming of Christ*, not a literal seven-year period.) Our headlines today are full of increasing peril. We are seeing earthquakes, volcanoes, major wildfires, famines, floods, droughts, wars, epidemics, disease, pestilence, persecution, murderous dictators, genocides, sex trafficking, tornados and hurricanes, tsunamis, catastrophic disasters, violence, murder, and massive political unrest, deception, fraud, and outright lies. We will soon be living among the most unrighteous, self-centered, self-absorbed, self-indulgent, and perverse generation who ever lived. I believe it's looking like this right now.

The Church has most certainly lived through tribulation and "dark ages" in the past, and has been refined, purged, and proved by God during extremely difficult times in *every* generation. *We* will be purged and refined as well. A child of God must be willing to bear suffering, shame, and death for Christ, and rejoice that he is counted worthy of it. We are not to fear the *consequences of our faithfulness*. God's people are required to be *faithful* to Him *despite* their surroundings and circumstances. Our generation does *not* get an exception to this rule.

Hebrews 13:8 says that God is the *same* yesterday, today, and forever. We read accounts in scripture where God *immediately* destroyed careless and disobedient people right on the spot, but *today* we see unprecedented blasphemy, idolatry, and every sort of debauchery, with no apparent consequence from God above. Because it is rare to see God's *immediate* judgment today, people have come to believe that God has changed. The earth-dwellers relate to God as being *all* patient and merciful, kind and tolerant, because His punishment of the unredeemed, command-ment-breaking wicked rebels is being *reserved* and *deferred*. But be *assured, God's anger at sin has not changed.* He is long-suffering and merciful, giving all people ample opportunity and time to repent. God's clemency is available to *everyone* who repents and comes to Jesus for salvation.

But—*no* unrighteousness, unrepentant, rebel will *ever* stand innocently or ignorantly before God. Even the seemingly *deceived* are not innocent victims. They *choose* darkness as opposed to righteousness and light. They know right from wrong. They *refuse* clemency.

> **Romans 1:20** For the invisible things of him from the cre-
> ation of the world *are clearly seen*, being understood by the
> things that are made, even his eternal power and Godhead;
> so that *they are without excuse:*

At the end of time on earth, the guilty, unrighteous enemies of
God will gather in *battle* against the Lord. The Antichrist himself, with all his evil forces, will *lead* and *deceive* them. Do not be
fearful. If you are in right standing with God, don't worry that
the Antichrist will deceive *you.* No righteous person has ever
been suddenly overcome with deception. The deceived doubt
God, have *rebellious* hearts, and lack necessary God-pleasing
faith. It is their own *free-will choice* to shun God's light. They
do *not* cling to the *only* hope of their rescue, Jesus Christ. Not
knowing God's Word is dangerously close to not knowing God.
Without the hope of *God's truth* to stand on, it is unlikely that
one will stand. Intentional and personal study of the Word of
God, to better know God, is *imperative* for all believers. John
17:25 says it is *the world* who does not know God. The world,
here, means the earth-dwellers.

At the end of time, the devil is going to lead a major uprising
against God in one final battle, called Armageddon. God gloriously wins and destroys all evildoers in this futile conflict,
casting them into hell, *forever.* Evil will *never* flaunt its ugly
face before God again. You can take that to the bank.

> **Nahum 1:9** What do ye imagine against the LORD? he will
> make an utter end: *affliction shall not rise up the second time.*

God is *not ever* going to let the devil out of hell and give him
another shot at Him and at His family. The second coming of

Christ concludes the symbolic millennium. There is no more death—ever. The devil has already had his last big hurrah in the millennium and at the end of it in the battle of Armageddon. He loses. God's people will eternally and securely live in God's perfect kingdom when the new heaven and new earth come down and unite. God's own presence will be with the saints forever. There is *no sin* in God's kingdom. The devil will *never* get out of hell to rise up a second time and take a second shot at God's people.

In concert with the huge miscalculation of the timing of the rapture, the Church has also miscalculated the timing of the *millennium*. For this reason, many believe that the devil will be released from hell to come back against God's people *one more time* at the end of a thousand years of peace in God's perfect kingdom. That would mean Satan would one day be allowed to have access to God's perfect kingdom and His rescued people. *Not on your life.*

Jesus Christ has a kingdom *now*, in the intermediate heaven. The devil has *no access* to it, and he *never* will. Believer's souls are transported to this intermediate state, *Paradise,* when they die. John sees a vision of *the living martyrs in the intermediate heaven*, and he calls this *the first resurrection* (Rev. 20:4–5). This is a vision of the revival of dead saints, not the unregenerated dead. John then goes back, in his style of writing with *flashbacks*, and informs about the *end* of the millennium of the entire Church age, and the final war, Gog and Magog. *This is the millennium that we live in.* Satan is temporarily *loosed* from being bound at the end of *this* millennium, just prior to the day of the Lord. After he claims his final victims and rises up in his final affront against God, he gets his just deserts. He is cast alive into the lake of fire, and *he will never be loosed out of his prison again.*

For the modern-day understanding of the thousand-year future millennium to be correct, death would actually *not* be conquered at the second coming of Christ. Evil would necessarily continue among the saints in God's perfect kingdom after the saints are *securely* living in the presence of God and during the time when Satan is abiding in hell. That is in *no* way scriptural. It is also rather unsettling.

On the last day, at the Lord's second coming, Satan and all the resurrected bodies of the *unrighteous*, along with *the living unrighteous* earth-dwellers, will be cast alive into hell, which is a *permanent* place for their punishment and destruction. These will *remain* in torment for all eternity. No one is ever coming out of hell.

Nothing in scripture says that people procreate in their *glorified* bodies. There is no marriage in heaven. Evil does not show up in the *perfect* kingdom of God, requiring the devil to be released to claim more victims. What victims is he going to claim? That is *very* misguided theology. No, there will be no disobedient *children* growing up in heaven. The kingdom that comes down with Jesus and the saints is the *new* heaven. *It is secure!*

Remember, the millennium is a *symbolic* period of time which started with the Church age and ends with the second coming of Christ. At the *end* of the millennium, just before the return of Christ, God's restraint on Satan's power and freedom of action will be lifted for a brief time until the final day of wrath.

Currently, Satan operates out of the abyss. The abyss is not the same as the lake of fire described in Revelation 19 and 20. It is sometimes called the bottomless pit. Disembodied unrighteous souls of the damned are held there, along with legions of demons. The righteous dead, however, go to the intermediate heaven, Paradise, to await their complete redemption and glorified bodies.

Hell is for the unrighteous, every one of whom would be a full-blown Satan if the seed of *their own sin* would come to full fruition. Hell was not created for those who follow God. God calls His faithful servants, kings and priests who are blessed and holy. He said we will *never* suffer the second death—eternal separation from him. He said we would shed *no more tears* once we were in his eternal kingdom. Should we imagine, then, that God's holy, redeemed saints would one day suffer the loss of millennial children right out of God's perfect, eternal kingdom where there are no more tears? God forbid. No devil is getting out of hell to have *a second uprising* among those living securely in the presence of Jesus Christ.

> **Revelation 21:4** And God shall wipe away all tears from their eyes; and there shall be no more death, neither sorrow, nor crying, neither shall there be any more pain: for the former things are passed away.

If God opened up hell, for the devil to come out and claim more victims after a thousand years, then the second death, which is eternal separation from God, would be a reality *once again*. Death would *not* have been conquered at the second coming of Christ. That is unscriptural. There is *no* sin in God's eternal kingdom, and nothing there is accursed, nor ever will be. God's people are joined together with Him in unity. No one is having children who wander off into rebellion and sin in this kingdom. That would cause sorrow. Stop the unscriptural nonsense.

When Christians are called up to meet the Lord in the air, the earth will be utterly destroyed by God. A new heaven and new earth will be created and united, thus ending the division between God and man. God will bring the redeemed back to His restored, original, perfect creation, before the fall of man. The first book of the Bible, in Genesis 2, the author, Moses, shows us the garden of Eden with the Tree of Life in the midst of the garden and the Tree of the Knowledge of Good and Evil. God walked with Adam and Eve in this garden. At the end of biblical text, in Revelation, God's final words to the Church, we are shown that the all the rescued saints will dwell with God where the Tree of Life grows. We are going to Eden.

Revelation 20 portrays Christ's heavenly reign *right now*, not in the future. Christ has an intermediate kingdom right *now*. That is why we pray, "Thy kingdom come." There most certainly will be a new heaven and new earth, and the people of God will walk and talk with Jesus on safe streets. There will be no sorrow and pain, ever again.. This is the eternal kingdom we call heaven.

Revelation 20 is *not* the chronological continuation of Revelation 19. This controversial "millennium" chapter requires deep and dedicated study and meditation. It has been hotly debated by Bible scholars over the centuries. I implore *you* to study Revelation 20, to see if you think what I have said is true. I might have to write another book to highlight the biblical context of my conclusion that *the millennium is now*. Be a Berean, and study for yourself. I pray that you will arrive at the truth.

CHAPTER 2

The Church's Report Card—
Not Looking So Good

Revelation, unlike the other sixty-five books in the Bible, is *primarily* focused on what is *about* to happen on the earth as the result of mankind (earth-dwellers) coming to the end of *self-rule*. Self-rule is the rejection of *God's* rulership. It is the sinful, selfish, and prideful way of the devil who wants to *usurp* God's authority. Lucifer and one third of the angelic realm rejected the ways of God and were cast from heaven (Ezek. 28:13–19). All created beings who reject the rulership of God bring judgment upon themselves and will ultimately face eternal separation from God. Time ticks away, allowing every person an opportunity to choose sides.

Christian ideals are vanishing before our very eyes. Human tragedy and danger are increasing at startling rates. Every day on the news and in our communities, we see evidence of man's godless self-rule. We witness hatred and hostility toward everything good and holy. We hear of mayhem and murder, crime, chaos, blasphemy, perversion, lies, and deception. We observe blasphemy, contempt, idolatry, incurable disobedience, and unbelief against God our Creator. Few people today are seeking God and inquiring of Him. They are just not interested. God is *irrelevant* to many in our contemporary culture. God is cursed daily without hesitation by irreverent, arrogant, and prideful sinners. Persecution against God's people, along with censoring of truth and acts of violence against the innocent are on a wild upswing.

"God talk" is off limits. Don't bring that religious talk to the table or anywhere else for that matter. Today, the only acceptable "god" is the god of tolerance. The only accepted absolute, is that there are *no* absolutes. It is asserted that there is *no* truth, and there are *no* right answers. "*Do your own thing.*" Satan has convinced most people to serve their *self*-interests above everything. The multitudes make their own decisions about what is right and wrong, independent of the Word and will of God. Mankind has fallen victim to the devil's "apples," the pride of life, loving their own beauty, accomplishments, material possessions, positions, status, and even their immoral attractions and actions.

Even many professing Christians are undisciplined, and suffer from a *lack of desire* and readiness to know their God and do His will. Some give God a little "lip service" with rote meal prayers and one minute "bless my family" bedtime prayers. These one-minute prayers frequently serve as the entire day's "communion" with God, and are mostly supplications for God to bless those who are named in their prayers. Longer prayers are just so difficult, and the Church is lazy and preoccupied. We rarely commune with God in *focused* prayers during our *best* time of the day, but mostly pray during the last few minutes before our weary minds drift off into sleep. Do we remember to praise and worship God, confess our faults and sins, and thank

Him for His manifold benefits and blessings, or do we mostly just ask for His blessings and things we want and need?

How are we doing in reading and studying the Word of God as a part our daily life? In a Christian family, the *man* is supposed to be a "covering" for his wife. But why are so many Christian men failing to lead their families in prayer and in the study of God's Word? Where is the regular reading of God's Word, followed by discussion and prayer with the spouse or family? There is no time for it. We use our time for making money, career work, social media, the internet, the TV, yardwork, a hobby, and the busyness of life.

> **1 Peter 4:18** And if the righteous *scarcely* be saved, where shall the ungodly and the sinner appear?

It is starting to look like the Church is clearly guilty of self-serving lifestyles, just like the rest of the world. *Our* interests are over *God's* interests. In accepting and daily practicing the standards and lifestyles of our contemporary culture, (loving the world) many professing Christians are actually borderline to full-on counterfeits. God looks on the heart and easily observes when one's mouth is out of step with their actions. Secret sins, pride, hostilities, presumptuousness, unforgiveness, self-will, and lukewarmness are *not* hidden to God. God is an omniscient Spirit, and He is omnipresent. He knows all things, at all times, about all people. We just have *no* idea.

> **Job 36:26a** Behold, God *is* great, and *we know him not*

> **1 John 2:15** Love not the world, neither the things that are in the world. If any man love the world, the love of the Father is not in him.

It is important, that we get a clear picture of *ourselves* and our contemporary culture *before* we study the book of Revelation. It is also important to understand that the *physical* universe in which we live is sustained by the *spiritual* world where the Spirit of God dwells. Because we are physical beings, our understanding of the spiritual universe is *limited* to our thoughts, which are filtered by what is physical. *Only God can reveal that which is spiritual to man.* In revealing the invisible, spiritual things of God to man, *God's Word often uses the physical to teach about the spiritual* because humans are limited to the physical universe in this present age.

When Jesus Christ became a physical man and walked among mankind, He often taught what is spiritual to His followers, using physical examples and symbols. *Jesus spoke in spiritual symbolism to the people.*

> **John 6:51** "I am the living bread which came down from heaven: if any man eat of this bread, he shall live forever: and the bread that I will give is my flesh, which I will give for the life of the world."

> **John 6:54** "*Whoever eats My flesh and drinks My blood* has eternal life, and I will raise him up at the last day."

Because spiritual symbolism is too difficult for mankind to understand on his own, Jesus often told His disciples the meaning of the symbols. *Those who would genuinely listen to*

Jesus with the desire to obey the truth, would begin to "see" truth through the mind of the Spirit. God is still opening "spiritual eyes" today when anyone hears His Word with the intention to obey revealed truth.

In Jesus's time on earth, those who could not get beyond the *physical* did not comprehend what Jesus taught because they got hung up over his use of *spiritual symbolism* in their physical world. They could not receive true spiritual understanding. *Skeptics* stopped following Him altogether. Others, not understanding what Christ taught, made *religious* attempts to "follow" by adopting the physical symbols He used to teach with.

Jesus spoke *symbolically* of eating His flesh and blood. Those who *did not understand spiritually* what Christ was saying began attempting to serve God by taking physical elements *and considering it an actual sacrifice of Christ's real flesh and blood.* God was offering something far greater, yet the *spiritually blind* began practicing *religious idolatry* and *limiting* the eternally existent, omnipotent Creator of all that is visible and invisible to a physical, decomposing fragment of bread and a cup of fermented grape juice. They would *imagine* to be able to call God down to enter their bread "*sacrifice,*" which they imagined to be *God's flesh* to be eaten by them. Great *religious deception* rests on all those who *will not,* and therefore *cannot,* understand *spiritual symbols.* They are limited to the physical because their *hearts* are *not* open to God's truth.

Unregenerated mankind, in his physical nature, *rejects* true knowledge of a spiritual God. Yet God woos and calls those who *will* receive him *in spirit and in truth* to come out of the world and into new life. This "new life" comes from God alone.

(No earthly memberships are involved at all.) This new life is a "new birth," and is called being "born again." This is when a person becomes a part of God's spiritual body and joins God's eternal family. This born-again person, unlike the lost, is able to come to know God through His inspired, written Word *and understand* His *spiritual* purpose and mission in this physical world. All those who are *not* called by God are *unable* to know who God truly is. They *cannot* know God's purpose and mission on earth. They are limited, and even prohibited, in spiritual understanding *unless God* opens their eyes. These are the lost and yet may be very religious people.

These are the spiritually blind and dead. These physical mortals have no eternal connection to God's truth and His kingdom. In their misguided beliefs, they deny God as the moral governor of the world, giving their earthly leaders and rulers equal footing. They place their impotent God in the same category as any common idol. These blind and lost are "*earth-dwellers*" and are *not* God's peculiar people, consecrated to His service. They actually despise "the narrow way" and the *simple* way of *faith and grace.* They are the *lost.* They seek to follow other teachers and leaders who add to and subtract from the truths in the holy scriptures.

The deceived, *religious* earth-dwellers are *counterfeits.* Many even declare themselves to be Christians, but none of them accept the all-sufficient and *finished* work of Jesus Christ on the Cross of Calvary. They seek to establish their *own* righteousness through obedience to the laws, rules, traditions, and customs of earthly leaders and religious groups. They seek to enter heaven apart from grace alone, through faith alone, and are therefore "under the law" and have never been saved by God's grace.

Romans 4:4 Now to him who works, the wages are not counted as grace but as debt.

It is necessary to see and understand spiritual things through spiritual eyes. The whole book of Revelation is written in *spiritual*, apocalyptic, and *symbolic* language.

Revelation 1:1 The Revelation of Jesus Christ, which God gave unto him, to shew unto his servants things which must shortly come to pass; and he sent and *signified* it by his angel unto his servant John:

People who *genuinely* seek God, *will* have their *spiritual* eyes opened by God. If one's *spiritual eyes* are *not* opened by God, he will *not* be able to understand anything spiritual. The Word of God is *not* understood intellectually, but spiritually. So, the first order of business when studying biblical text and commentary is to *pray* and *ask God for wisdom* to understand *His* Word and to know *Him* in *spirit and in truth.*

The purpose of this book is to help expose what is true and what is false about contemporary beliefs regarding the last days of time. The Church must be *properly prepared* to stand firm and follow Jesus Christ through the *difficult times ahead.* Satan has pulled off a deceptive scheme of making the modern church unaware of their need to suffer and deny themselves for the cause and mission of Christ. It is only when our self-will is fully surrendered to *Christ* and we are fully dependent on Him that we will fully stand in the *power* of Christ to overcome the wicked spiritual influences of culture and society. If we don't strip every attachment we have to the enemy's system, we will be weak, worldly, and preoccupied with things that distract us from God's purposes. God wants to use *us* to carry out *His* mission in the earth during these last days.

We all need to be challenged about how deeply committed to Christ we really are. Would we ask God to do *whatever it takes* in our lives to make us more like Him? That's a scary thought because we are probably *all* "missing the mark" in areas of our lives, and we know it. We tend to be somewhat dishonest with ourselves about our true condition of spiritual health. We have work to do. God wants our steadfast love, our dependence on him alone, and He wants us to be his unashamed and faithful witnesses in the earth. How are we doing?

CHAPTER 3

The Body of Christ— One Family

In our study of the book of Revelation, we will consider the content as if we were in the early church to whom it was written. It is most likely that we would *not* possess our own personal copy of the scriptures back in John's day because each copy had to be hand-written on scrolls. God's Word would come to us through his prophets, like John and Paul and the apostles.

Revelation, while written to the *seven* churches in Asia, is also written *to* and *for all* of God's servants, the whole house of God. *Every* chapter of Revelation is for the Church's instruction, admonition, and warning, as well as for encouragement and exhortation. Every problem addressed to the seven churches of Asia is representative of all the problems seen in all of God's family of believers in the same way that God's Ten Commandments are representative of *all* sin to be avoided.

It is unwise to shrink the Bible to *our* level, eliminating sections as unprofitable and unmeaningful—written for *someone else's* instruction, not ours. The *entire* Bible is written for *all* mankind.

The Bible is sacred text, and it forbids cutting any words from it. The Bible is a true recording of facts that *have* happened and that *are going to* happen. Nevertheless, many students of the Bible are guilty of reading the book of Revelation and assigning the greater portion of it to be relevant to *another* group of people, not including themselves. It's not a comfortable book.

It is certain that most of us have viewed the bizarre and frightening events in Revelation as futuristic and definitely not something that will happen to *us* in *our* lifetime. Many Christians have been taught to read Revelation like: "Chapters 1–3, are written to the Asian churches, and we certainly can find elements of our own churches in these verses, but the rest of the chapters are for the 'end-time tribulation saints' who are a future group of select Jews."

Are you willing to face the possibility that we have been *wrong*, and these bizarre and frightening events are maybe not so futuristic and are more *symbolic* than literal. They may even be in *our* lifetime. Maybe the symbolic visions of John the Revelator actually look more like things we are seeing today, and don't recognize because we have clung to *literal* interpretations, and we are thinking of scary, demonic-looking animals, bugs, and beasts. Though Revelation is a rather frightening and strange book, every word of it is God-authored, and is meaningful for *all* of the Church. The unusual order of Revelation is not a mistake. John recorded his visions in the order *God* gave him. Although difficult, it is wise for all of us to carefully contemplate *the final message and plea from God to us—before* His pre-ordained, cataclysmic *end to all rebellion* begins full swing.

There are no other books in the Bible where we would read and differentiate between the first few chapters and the rest of the chapters, as if they were written to a *different* audience. Revelation has *one* audience: the *complete* Church. God does not have two different families.

The early followers of Jesus Christ did not have any reason to believe that most of the book of Revelation was written to some *other* far-in-the-future group of *select Jewish people*. Verse 3 of John's first letter to the Asian churches informs that "the time is at hand." His audience would not have assumed, "Most of the Revelation that God gave to John has no significance to us because it is in the distant future and is unrelated to Gentile Christians. We won't be here anyway." *No.* They would have *never* come to that conclusion from John's letters, so it would be wise for us to understand that this *not* what they believed. You can't find *anywhere* in scripture that the early Church believed in our modern-day, made-up scenario about *two* second comings. Revelation is all about *one* second coming of Christ. His followers were not just Jews. They were *believers*, so they were *Christians*.

All the people on earth who are *not* ready for the second coming of Christ will experience Christ's second coming as a "thief in the night." This is *not* meant to be *a saying* about the *timing* of Christ's return, but about *how one should live* in light of his return. This will be a *rescue* to the *ready*, but God's wrath awaits all those rebels who are *not*. John Specifically informed the seven churches of Asia that the things in this prophecy and the time of tribulation was *"at hand."* Therefore, the early Church considered *all* of John's prophecy as meaningful to *them*. They were informed to be watchful and intentional in serving God.

Rev. 1:3 for the time is at hand.

Rev. 3:11 Behold, I come quickly

Rev. 16:15 Behold, I come as a thief. Blessed is he that watcheth

Rev. 22:6 which must shortly be done.

Rev. 22:7 Behold, I come quickly

Rev. 22:10 for the time is at hand.

Rev. 22:12 behold, I come quickly

Rev. 22:20 Surely I come quickly

Prior to John's writings of Revelation, the apostle Paul had also written about the end, to the Thessalonians. He stated that *the day of Christ is at hand*, and he told them of a *sign* that would precede *that day*.

> **2 Thessalonians 2:1-3** Now we beseech you, brethren, by the coming of our Lord Jesus Christ, and by our gathering together unto him, That ye be not soon shaken in mind, or be troubled, neither by spirit, nor by word, nor by letter as from us, as that the day of Christ is at hand. Let no man deceive you by any means: for that day shall not come, except there come a falling away first, and that man of sin be revealed, the son of perdition;

When John finished writing the Revelation of Jesus Christ, he didn't bury it in a time capsule and hope that the future followers of Jesus did *not* find it and think it was meant for *them*. He did not write the first three chapters and then start a different book with a different audience. There weren't even chapter divisions at the time he recorded his prophetic visions. *All* of Revelation was written to the audience God chose: *the universal and complete Church of Jesus Christ.* The number seven in scripture symbolizes *complete*.

The seven churches in Revelation include all of the redeemed Jews (twelve tribes) and all of the redeemed Gentiles (twelve apostles). The number 1,000 is typically *symbolic* of a multitude, or very large number ($12 \times 12 \times 1,000$) or $12 \times 12 \times$ *the multitude.* $12 \times 12 \times 1,000$ = 144,000). *This is symbolic of the complete Church from every age.*

The particular commendations, challenges, and indictments aimed at each of the seven churches are not characteristic of only these seven local churches. There are many individual characteristics in every body of believers, which congregate in physical churches and in communities across the world. Any interpretation that limits the commendations, challenges, and warnings to these seven specific local churches, or to those church types only, does not understand the figurative nature of John's apocalyptic language. *John's warnings are prophetic and timeless.* He was addressing the *whole* house of God, in every age, with individual applications. *All* born-again individuals make up the house of God, or 'the Church.' If an individual child of God sees his own personal characteristic faults mentioned in *any* of John's indictments to the seven churches, whether in one specific church only, or in several, this individual needs to make the corrections that John implores, or he will receive the corrections that John prophecies. All of the conditions in the seven churches have existed in the local churches since the beginning of the Church. Believers are called to overcome these conditions and repent of sin.

The Seven Churches = The Whole Body of Christ = All the Righteous Believers

> **Romans 10:4** For Christ is the end of the law for righteousness to *every one that believeth.*

Romans 10:12 For there is *no difference* between the Jew and the Greek: for the same Lord over all is rich unto all that call upon him.

Romans 11:17 You Gentiles are like branches of a wild olive tree made to be part of a cultivated olive tree. You have taken the place of some branches that were cut away from it. And because of this, you enjoy the blessings that come from being part of that cultivated tree.

John 10:16 I have other sheep that are not of this fold. I must bring them in as well, and they will listen to My voice. Then there will be *one flock* and one shepherd.

Romans 11:24 For if you were cut from a wild olive tree, and contrary to nature *were grafted into one* that is cultivated, how much more readily will these, the natural branches, be grafted into their own olive tree.

There is only one true church.

One flock
One salvation
One shepherd
One, not two.
One.

The Jews do *not* have a separate salvation, different from the Gentiles. There is *one* family of God. One body.

Ephesians 3-6 How that by revelation he made known unto me *the mystery*; (as I wrote afore in few words, Whereby, when ye read, ye may understand my knowledge in *the mystery of Christ*) Which in other ages was not made known unto the sons of men, as it is *now revealed* unto his holy apostles and prophets by the Spirit...That the Gentiles should be fellow heirs, and of *the same body,* and partakers of his promise in Christ by the gospel:

Acts 17:26-28 And hath made *of one blood* all nations of men for to dwell on all the face of the earth, and hath determined the times before appointed, and the bounds of their habitation; That they should seek the Lord, if haply they might feel after him, and find him, though he be not far from every one of us: For in him we live, and move, and have our being; as certain also of your own poets have said, *For we are also his offspring.*

The body of Christ was actually conceived and formed by God before the foundation of the world (Eph. 1:4), not on Pentecost. The Church, which is the body of Christ, will not be complete until it is presented to Christ on the *last day. All* of the people who have been saved by the grace of Jesus Christ are "the chosen," the adopted children of God, the called-out people, the Church, whether Jew or Gentile by birth. *And, there is no separate group of believers in the tribulation period either.* You can take this paragraph to the bank.

Ephesians 1-5 Blessed be the God and Father of our Lord Jesus Christ, who hath blessed **us** with all spiritual blessings in heavenly places in Christ: According as *he hath chosen us in him before the foundation of the world*, that we should be holy and without blame before him in love: Having

> *predestinated us unto the adoption of children by Jesus Christ*
> *to himself,* according to the good pleasure of his will,

The early church did not begin as a mixture of the saved and unsaved, or true believers and pagan deceivers and hypocrites. There was too much persecution going on, and the way was too narrow for most people to casually and carelessly decide that they wanted to follow Jesus. Acts 5:13 says, *"Although the people regarded them (the apostles) highly, no one else dared to join them."* The stakes were high, and "membership" meant they would face rejection and suffering. Serious persecution and the scorn of the world kept the Church clean of hypocrites and deceivers for many decades. When persecutions eased up and ceased, more divisions and strife appeared in the Church, making it necessary for God's anointed prophets to write letters correcting the practices and doctrines of believers. One such writer is the apostle Paul.

The apostle Paul wrote letters to local churches, primarily because there were misunderstandings among the followers of Jesus Christ in personal matters, in doctrine, and in divine truths. Additionally, Paul wrote letters to the churches to address issues of *persecution* and false teachers. Paul's letters and the writings of God's inspired prophets were to not only reveal God's holy truths, but to reveal *the mission of God* in the world through His Son, Jesus Christ. *God's mission is to gather unto Christ, one faithful body, to enjoy with Him an endless future of righteousness and joy.* God is restoring heaven and earth to Himself and has overcome evil through the death and resurrection of Jesus Christ. *God is making the body of Christ one with Him.*

God spoke to His people in the early Church through His chosen vessels, the apostles and disciples. The inspired words were recorded on scrolls and then later written in book form for the followers of Jesus Christ in *every* age. God's words are bound together in our inspired and preserved holy Bibles. We need to regularly read these inspired words.

As previously stated, the writings of John's inspired visions in the book of Revelation were not specific to the first-century churches only. There were many more congregations of the Church of God in the first century than those seven: Rome, Lystra, Corinth, Philippi, and Colossae, just to name a few more. John's words were for them as well—and also for the Church *today.* Imagine reading: "He that hath an ear, let him hear what the Spirit saith unto the Churches," and saying, *"I think I'll just skip that part because it was only written to seven Asian churches back in the day. It's not for the Church today."* Wrong.

What John wrote to the Asian churches complements what God had already addressed to His universal body of believers through Paul. John's letters to the seven churches did not nullify any other messages from God to the Church. John's letters to the seven churches, like many of Paul's letters, contained directives and warnings. However, the difference is the warnings in *John's* letters are meant to be *final warnings* and a plea from God for sinners and nominal Christians to repent. They are prophetic of the period of time that precedes God's final judgment against all sin *at his coming.*

Revelation is a book about the end of the world *and the rapture.* It is about that day when Christ is glorified in the saints. Much of the book of Revelation is about this one day, the day of the second coming of the Lord. The culminating events of the Revelation of Jesus Christ depict a spectacular scene where *all* of God's armies and *all* of the saints in heaven are descending from heaven *with* Jesus Christ. On *that day*, all of the dead in Christ will rise from their graves to meet Jesus and His company in the clouds. The saints who are still alive on earth will also rise to meet the Lord in the air. When *all* the righteous saints meet with the Lord in the air, God avenges his beloved bride, *the complete Church,* by pouring out His wrath on all the unrighteous, unrepentant sinners on earth, bringing an *end* to sin and every form of evil *forever*. On that day, God is glorified in the saints. It is that day when the last enemy, death, is put under foot.

While not the main theme or point of this book, we will necessarily examine scripture and see that there is *no* scriptural validity for a *pretribulation* rapture belief. The pretribulation belief demands belief in: *two* second comings, an *early* harvest, and the church separated from the rest of the world *before* the "wheat" and "tares" are separated. Pretribulation belief teaches that a group of Christians is guaranteed complete inoculation from end-of-days tribulation and suffering, via a *secret*, quiet rapture. This position teaches that the *last* trumpet, which precedes this event, isn't really the last trumpet, and earth-dwellers won't hear it. (It's a *quiet* trumpet.) There are *seven more* trumpets to go because at the second coming of Christ, *another* seventh trumpet is blown.

Pretribulationists teach that Christians will dine with Christ in a carnal banquet "wedding feast" in heaven that *excludes* 144,000 sealed Jews who are actually God's *newly saved* children but left behind to witness to sinners. This theory teaches that these sealed *Jews* are separated from Christians and are still on earth, being slaughtered, and will never get to participate in the Marriage Supper of the Lamb. The pretribulation belief demands a last day for the Church, *plus* seven more years for *the rest of the body* (the sealed Jews) who are still on earth. The pretribulation belief has saints getting glorified bodies in a rapture seven years *prior to* the day of the Lord when Christ is glorified in the saints at his *coming*. This belief also demands a rapture seven years *prior to* the *first resurrection* of "*those who sleep in Jesus," which would actually make this rapture an early harvest.* Then, *after* this *early* harvest, *a new crop*, the Jews who suffer in the tribulation, are harvested. Pretribulationists believe that *no* judgment commences for seven years after the rescue of the first "crop" of saints. They believe that the *day of Lord* is actually a *third* coming, but they don't *call* it that *because they don't count the second coming as a "coming"* because Jesus's *feet* didn't touch the earth in the secret, stealthy, second coming (*not called a "coming" because of where His feet were.*) Oh my, I'm getting dizzy.

Really? Are you kidding me? The church has been fed a big fat lie. This is *not* scriptural at all. Repent of this nonsensical and unscriptural man-made lie. These scenarios *cannot* be found in scripture, nor in any writing of the early church fathers prior to 1830. It is around that time that the suggestion of *two separate harvests,* one for the saved Gentiles and one for the Jews, was presented to the believers by a misguided author and preacher named *John Darby.* Many more writers and teachers then jumped on that "bandwagon," adding this *false* doctrine to their creed, catechism, and statements of faith. Darby erroneously taught that God had a different fate for the Jewish people and for the Christian Church. You can read the history of Darby's false doctrines in quite a number of other books and resources, so I will not go into it here.

People clinging to the early harvest, secret rapture theory, typically will dismiss the *clear* teachings *of scripture* and claim that *the words do not mean what they say.* A number of popular pretribulation books devote entire chapters to explain why the clear words of prophetic scripture don't really mean what they say. They claim that most of the book of Revelation is not written *to* and *for* the Church. They implore our belief of *their* interpretations, built on faulty suppositions, inferences, and twisted words. They hold tight to their faulty interpretations *in the absence of any clear proof texts* that depict the rapture as quiet and secret, and happening *before* the final separation of wheat and tares at the *end* of the world.

In Christ's own words, in the "red letter" section of the Bible, He specifically emphasized that His return would be a *glorious, visible, loud*, and a *dramatic* event. Christ's own description of His return should be the final word on whether He returns silently and secretly or *visible to all*.

> **Matthew 24:26-27** Wherefore if they shall say unto you, Behold, he is in the desert; go not forth: behold, he is in the secret chambers; believe it not. For *as the lightning* cometh out of the east, and shineth even unto the west; so shall also the coming of the Son of man be.

Lightning is visible. Jesus was warning the church to *not* fall prey to any claim that His coming would be secret and subtle. Jesus was literally answering His disciples questions, "Tell us, *when* shall these things be? and what shall be the sign of thy coming, and of the end of the world?" (Mark 13:3b). Jesus informed that the very day of His epiphany will *not* be concealed but will be a very bright, very loud, very glorious, and a very public event. "There will be a "*loud* command," "the voice of the archangel," and "the trumpet call *of God*" at His appearing. *These are not presented to represent silence.*

Can you imagine Christ coming to rescue His bride from all His enemies, and He gets *no glory* in that day? Say what? The bride's rescue is secret and invisible, quiet and subtle, and then *seven years later* He comes *again* at the *end* of tribulation, and *another* "last trumpet" sounds when God rescues the second crop, the Jews, who went through the tribulation while His favored bride, the Christians, dined with Him in heaven and enjoyed their new celestial surroundings for a few years while the Jews on the earth (God's favored people) got threatened, punished, terrorized, starved, plagued, and beheaded? What nonsense.

What Jesus Christ Himself said about that day undermines this whole invisible rapture *theory*, which divides the body of Christ into two groups. Christ and all His angels do *not* descend from heaven, tiptoeing like stealth bandits and wearing muzzles over their mouths. The Bible teaches that Christ *appears (epiphaneia)*, and that *His appearing is our blessed hope.* (Titus 2:13) This *visible* day of Christ's *appearing* is the day we are to be looking for, *not* a different day with a silent, secret removal from the earth. *Every* eye will see God's rescue of His people, so why would anyone believe this to be a silent, secret snatching away?

> **Titus 2:13** *Looking for* that blessed hope, and the glorious *appearing* of the great God and our Saviour Jesus Christ;

The rapture will come *after* tribulation. No scripture says that the complete measure of tribulation judgment is at the very end of time and limited to seven years right before the return of Christ. God has been getting mankind's attention and calling him to repentance through judgments on the land, sea, and fresh waters *over all time.* Redemptive judgments are *not* just reserved for a final seven-year period. Saints have lived through the times of God's redemptive judgments since the beginning of creation.

The whole Bible is the story of God's redemption plan. In the *end* of this age, the mystery of God will be complete, and God will have *one* people for Himself, to dwell with in eternity—*one people.* Together, *all faithful believers* make up the true Church.

In studying the book of Revelation, we must ask, "What is God saying to the Church in every age, and specifically, what is God saying to *us*, the last day's Church?" Here is something which God inspired John to emphasize at least *eight* times, so I think it is very important. In the book of Revelation, John repeats one phrase prominently: "*him/he that overcometh*":

> **2:7** To him *that overcometh* will I give to eat of the tree of life ...

> **2:11** He *that overcometh* shall not be hurt of the second death.

> **2:17** To him *that overcometh* will I give to eat of the hidden manna...

> **2:26** And he *that overcometh*, and keepeth my works unto the *end*

> **3:5** He *that overcometh*, the same shall be clothed in white raiment...

> **3:12** Him *that overcometh* will I make a pillar in the temple of my God...

3:21 To him *that overcometh* will I grant to sit with me in my throne...

21:7 He *that overcometh* shall inherit all things; and I will be his God, and he shall be my son.

John details exactly what *overcoming* entails. It is the means by which we conquer evil, as God's holy people. Here it is. *We* will conquer the dragon.

> And they *overcame* him by the blood of the Lamb,
> and by the word of their testimony; and they loved
> not their lives unto the death.
> Revelation 12:11

CHAPTER 4

A Summary of the Judgments Leading up to the Symbolic Last Day

I will not include the *last day* judgments in this summary, as we'll arrive at *that day* later in the book.

<u>SEALS 1–5</u> These are meant to be *redemptive*.

The seal judgments depict how God brings redemptive judgments to all unbelieving, wicked, and rebellious earth-dwellers in order to correct them and turn them from their sin. God corrects His redeemed children as well, because we go wandering away from Him into sin. God chastens mankind for our own good. God's Word warns that people who forsake Him will be destroyed, and He desires that *none* would perish. The Son of God gave His own life to save all who would come to Him for forgiveness and mercy.

<u>Seal 1</u> Christ came, *conquering and to conquer*. (The Cross and the Gospel will conquer evil.) This is the foundation of God's

redemption plan. The rescue, or the rapture, is the *final* affair of God's redemptive mission of his eternal family. Seal 1 isn't really a judgment. It is *the foundation of mankind's rescue.*

<u>Seal 2</u> The *sword* of God's Word brings condemnation and doom to evildoers. The "sword" divides people and nations. *"There is no peace, saith the LORD, unto the wicked"* (Isa. 48:22). Jesus said that He did not come to bring earthly peace, but peace between God and man. Those who resist and forsake God are also at war with His family, Christians, on earth. They also have no love for the people of Jesus's homeland, Israel. Sometimes the terror and sufferings from these hate-filled wars, and frictions between family members and communities will turn people to God. He is always waiting with grace and mercy.

<u>Seal 3</u> This is a portrayal of *pain and suffering, scarcity, and disease,* when mankind casts away the guidance and grace of God. This seal is potentially upon us right now. It will increase to its final intensity, if a major financial collapse happens worldwide and a famine ensues as a result. Some will turn to God. Redemption is always God's plan, and He will receive all who turn to Him.

<u>Seal 4</u> This seal depicts *death* through *disease epidemics, viruses, and pestilence.* Historically, in such stressful times as these, many people yield their lives to God, and He will receive them. But hell will claim unrepentant rebels *en masse* at the end of time. It appears that this seal might be increasing in intensity, as we continue to get reports of *pandemic* deaths. God's mercy and grace is still available.

Seal 5 The servants of Christ are *persecuted and martyred*. This has been going on in every century since creation, and will happen *en masse* at the end of time.

Open Doors USA reports that one out of six Christians in Africa, one out of three Christians in Asia, and one out of twenty-one Christians in South America experience high levels of persecution. One in nine Christians worldwide experience high levels of persecution. That equates to 245 million Christians suffering in the top fifty World Watch List countries alone.[2]

TRUMPETS 1–6 These are seriously *punitive* judgments (and yet still *redemptive* until the witnesses are called up to meet the Lord in the air).

These judgments happen concurrently with the ongoing seal judgments at the time of the end. They greatly intensify in frequency and intensity as the last day approaches.

Trumpet 1 The vegetation of the earth is burned up in massive fires. This is a very devastating judgment, but there is still time for repentance. Many people will lose everything in these fires. The earth-dwellers will *only* find peace if they turn to God.

Trumpet 2 More than a quarter of sea life, but less than half, will die. Something huge will come down from God above and kill a massive amount of creatures in the ocean. This same ratio of ships, (1:3), that trade by sea will be destroyed in this judgment. It is very devastating.

Trumpet 3 This judgment comes down from God and is fiery like a burning star. When it hits the earth, the fresh waters become very bitter. A third of mankind is affected by this judgment, and many of the guilty earth-dwellers will die from the bitter water.

Trumpet 4 This judgment affects the sun, moon, and stars. Complete darkness will envelop the earth for around a third part of the day and night. This judgment will show that God is sovereign over *everything*. The sun is one of the major symbols of stability in our physical universe. There can be *no* stability without God. The Light of the World will give His saints His peace. God will *never* leave us, nor forsake us.

Pronouncement: "Woe, Woe, Woe to the inhabiters of the earth (earth-dwellers)."

The last three trumpets are woeful. They are very grievous. These are the three woes.

Trumpet 5 This judgment comes with physical torment, directly from Satan and demonic beings who are loosed on the earth right out of the pit of hell. They torment all the God-rejecting earth-dwellers with torture and pain, but God will not allow them to die. God **only** allows them to hurt those who are *not* His sealed children. God will *never* leave His people, nor forsake us.

Trumpet 6 This judgment includes fire, smoke, and brimstone that kills approximately one third of all the remaining unredeemed on earth. This fire comes from a massive army of terrifying beings, perhaps not all earthly beings. The object of their destruction is *not* the vegetation of the earth. They come to destroy *people* who are not the sealed of God, who *refuse* to repent of their murders, sorceries, fornication, and thefts.

During these seal and trumpet judgments, Satan increases in power in the world. He is embodied in a human man who rises up with deceitful, charismatic power. He is the Antichrist. *The earth-dwellers will not see him that way. He will be their hero.* The world will be in utter chaos, and the Antichrist will arise to *fix* things. He will bring a semblance of *peace* and some feasible-sounding answers (devoid of God) for all of man's problems. He will consider himself to be God. *There will be tremendous pressure to submit to him, even under threats of death.* Death *will* be carried out against *God's* people who will not submit to him, nor take his mark, nor worship him. But—God *will* be with us, and we are *not* to fear. The children of God will not be forsaken.

Again, while the seal and trumpet judgments are happening, the Church is still on earth. Remember Revelation 12:11. *We must conquer evil with* our Lord Jesus Christ, until the *last day*— the end. Guess what. It's *not* going to be a picnic. We will be mocked, hated, and killed. Our "judgment" and persecution will come from the wrath of *man* and the *devil, not God.* The devil is at war with God and God's redeemed family as well. Though Satan looks like he is "on top" and winning for a while, it will be *short*-lived.

When Seals 6 and 7, and Trumpet 7 all happen simultaneously, it's going to end as a *glorious day.* Things are going to happen *really fast!* Graves will open up, and the "two" dead witnesses (both redeemed Jews and Gentiles) all over the earth will wake up and rise up together with any living saints to meet the Lord in the air. *Every* grave will open up, and *all who ever lived will witness this day,* with all the armies in heaven and all of God's angels descending with Jesus and His bride. *It will be spectacular. It will be glorious.*

God *is going to avenge his children*, the saved, in front of the *whole* world—(all who ever lived) on the day of the Lord, also known as the day of the Lord's vengeance. God will be glorified in the saints on *that day*.

PART TWO

Revelation—Chapter By Chapter

A s we study this most important, final book of the Bible, I am *not* going to attempt to make it all *literal* because I can't. No one can. There are some things we aren't necessarily meant to understand through our physical eyes and understanding. The events and characters of Revelation are God-ordained allegory for *spiritual* relevance. Some symbols do have literal meanings behind them. Sometimes the interpretation of these symbols is found within Revelation or can be found elsewhere in the Bible, where the same symbols are used.

Here is an example of an interpretation of a symbol found within Revelation. The seven golden lampstands in Revelation 1:12 are symbols for the seven churches. We are told this interpretation in Revelation 1:20. In addition, here is an example of an interpretation of a symbol found elsewhere in the Bible. Jezebel is referenced in John's letter to the church of Thyatira. The interpretation of this figurative language will be found in the Old Testament books of 1 and 2 Kings. We find out in these books that Jezebel was the wicked wife of King Ahab who enticed God's people into sexual immorality and idolatry.

To fully understand Revelation, we must use the rest of the Bible. Revelation is the summation of God's eternal plan and mystery. The words of Revelation are God's *final* written words, or scripture, to mankind. Every word of this last scripture relates to the whole of *God's complete redemptive plan*, beginning with Genesis. It all ties together.

CHAPTER 5

The Revelation of Jesus Christ

Revelation 1

1 The Revelation of Jesus Christ, which God gave unto him, to shew unto his servants things which must shortly come to pass; and he sent and signified *it* by his angel unto his servant John:
2 Who bare record of the word of God, and of the testimony of Jesus Christ, and of all things that he saw.
3 Blessed *is* he that readeth, and they that hear the words of this prophecy, and keep those things which are written therein: for the time *is* at hand.

The early Church may or may not have considered the words of John: "*the time is at hand*" to mean "at any moment." John was encouraging the Church to watch for and eagerly wait for these things he prophesied of. God also told John, "These things *must shortly come to pass*," prompting John to communicate to the Church the *urgency* of living in personal preparation for their own end-of-life review before a holy God. These "at any moment" statements are not meant to be *sayings* about the *timing* of Christ's return, but about *how* one should live in *light* of his return. This very day, you or I could face the living God. No one is promised a tomorrow.

The pronounced *blessing* for reading, studying, and obeying this Revelation is meant for *us*, not just someone else a long time ago. The blessing is conditional, however. John informs that the reader/hearer must *keep* those things which are written therein; in other words, be obedient to the truth that is contained and revealed in this book.

4 John to the seven churches which are in Asia: Grace *be* unto you, and peace, from him which is, and which was, and which is to come; and from the seven Spirits which are before his throne;

Seven churches represents the *complete Church* and *seven Spirits* represents the *triune God*.

5 And from Jesus Christ, *who is* the faithful witness, *and* the first begotten of the dead, and the prince of the kings of the earth. Unto him that loved us, and washed us from our sins in his own blood, 6 And hath made us kings and priests unto God and his Father; to him *be* glory and dominion for ever and ever. Amen.

All of God's redeemed servants are represented by the, "*us*" in verses 5 and 6. We are called *kings* because we are in bondage to no man. We are called *priests* because we can go directly to God. (We need no middleman.) Upon death, saints go to *Paradise*, God's intermediate heaven, where they rule and reign with Christ, and await their glorified bodies and complete redemption at the rapture of the Church. God values the redeemed more than we will ever understand.

7 Behold, he cometh with clouds; and every eye shall see him, and they *also* which pierced him: and all kindreds of the earth shall wail because of him. Even so, Amen.

Christ comes with the *clouds*, visibly. He is surrounded with brilliant beauty, purity, angelic spirits, unrivaled power, and glory, and He is surrounded by *the saints, His bride*, the *New Jerusalem*, all brilliantly purified by being washed in His own blood. Every person ever created will observe this spectacular coming!

> **Revelation 21:2** And I John saw the *holy city, new Jerusalem*, coming down from God out of heaven, prepared as *a bride* adorned for her husband.

> **Revelation 21:9b-10** And there came unto me one of the seven angels which had the seven vials full of the seven last plagues, and talked with me, saying, Come hither, I will shew thee *the bride*, the Lamb's wife And he carried me away in the spirit to a great and high mountain, and shewed me *that great city, the holy Jerusalem, descending out of heaven* from God,

> **Revelation 3:12** Him that overcometh will I make a pillar in the temple of my God, and he shall go no more out: and I will write upon him the name of my God, and the name of *the city of my God, which is new Jerusalem, which cometh down out of heaven* from my God: and I will write upon him my new name.

> **Revelation 19:7-14** Let us be glad and rejoice, and give honour to him: for the marriage of the Lamb is come, and his wife hath made herself ready. And to her was granted

that she should be arrayed in fine linen, clean and white: for the fine linen is the righteousness of saints. And he saith unto me, Write, Blessed are they which are called unto the marriage supper of the Lamb. And he saith unto me, These are the true sayings of God. And I fell at his feet to worship him. And he said unto me, See thou do it not: I am thy fellow servant, and of thy brethren that have the testimony of Jesus: worship God: for the testimony of Jesus is the spirit of prophecy. And I saw heaven opened, and behold a white horse; and he that sat upon him was called Faithful and True, and in righteousness he doth judge and make war. His eyes were as a flame of fire, and on his head were many crowns; and he had a name written, that no man knew, but he himself. And he was clothed with a vesture dipped in blood: *and his name is called The Word of God.* And the armies which were in heaven followed him upon white horses, clothed in fine linen, white and clean.

In his numerous visions of *that day* when Christ is coming in the clouds, John saw *the New Jerusalem, the bride of Christ,* dressed in fine white linen, and thousands and thousands of God's armies, all descending from heaven together.

8 I am Alpha and Omega, the beginning and the ending, saith the Lord, which is, and which was, and which is to come, the Almighty.

This is John unveiling Jesus Christ as the eternal God.

9 I John, who also am your brother, and companion in tribulation, and in the kingdom and patience of Jesus Christ, was in the isle that is called Patmos, for the word of God, and for the testimony of Jesus Christ.

John was a "born-again" citizen of God's kingdom, yet he was in *much tribulation* for the Word of God and the testimony of Jesus Christ. John, just like his audience, faced tribulation to overcome evil, like *we* do. The early Church was birthed into tribulation, the ultimate end of which is the conquering of Satan. *None* of the Church is exempt from the necessity of overcoming the devil through *suffering* for Christ. All must be *willing* to die for Christ, just as Christ was willing to die for us.

10 I was in the Spirit on the Lord's day, and heard behind me a great voice, as of a trumpet,

11 Saying, I am Alpha and Omega, the first and the last: and, What thou seest, write in a book, and send *it* unto the seven churches which are in Asia; unto Ephesus, and unto Smyrna, and unto Pergamos, and unto Thyatira, and unto Sardis, and unto Philadelphia, and unto Laodicea.

12 And I turned to see the voice that spake with me. And being turned, I saw seven golden candlesticks;

13 And in the midst of the seven candlesticks *one* like unto the Son of man, clothed with a garment down to the foot, and girt about the paps with a golden girdle.

14 His head and *his* hairs *were* white like wool, as white as snow; and his eyes *were* as a flame of fire;

15 And his feet like unto fine brass, as if they burned in a furnace; and his voice as the sound of many waters.

16 And he had in his right hand seven stars: and out of his mouth went a sharp twoedged sword: and his countenance *was* as the sun shineth in his strength.

John says he was "*in the Spirit on the Lord's day.*" In this vision, John sees Jesus Christ in kingly apparel, wearing the garments of a high priest. These garments symbolize both of God's roles, as *King and Judge.* John sees His eyes as a flame of fire. Deuteronomy 4:24 says *"The Lord thy God is a consuming fire."* God has righteous anger against those who have *shunned* His grace and mercy. The majority of these last-day rebels are unredeemable, but God is not willing that any would perish.

What John sees in this first vision prompts him to warn, rebuke, affirm, and commend the different churches. John discloses consequences for disobedience and warns the *Church* to be faithful to Jesus Christ *to the end.* His primary message from God to the Church is, *"Repent."*

In verse 16, what comes out of God's mouth is the sword of his Word, a powerful tool that can inflict fatal damage to an enemy. Jesus said, *"Think not that I am come to send peace on earth: I came not to send peace but a sword"* (Matt. 10:34). The truth of God's spoken Word brings divisions in families, in churches, and in nations. No power on earth is like the sword of God's Word. The two-edged sword of God's Word exposes, convicts, separates, divides, and judges.

17 And when I saw him, I fell at his feet as dead. And he laid his right hand upon me, saying unto me, Fear not; I am the first and the last: 18 *I am* he that liveth, and was dead; and, behold, I am alive for evermore, Amen; and have the keys of hell and of death.

Jesus alone has the authority (*the keys*) to shut people out of heaven. This verse shows the Lord as having supreme control and unlimited authority over death and the invisible world of darkness. Christ alone, with this *metaphorical key,* will shut out of heaven *all* unbelievers for *all* of eternity. God does not carry a physical set of keys.

19 Write the things which thou hast seen, and the things which are, and the things which shall be hereafter;
20 The mystery of the seven stars which thou sawest in my right hand, and the seven golden candlesticks. The seven stars are the angels of the seven churches: and the seven candlesticks which thou sawest are the seven churches.

The seven stars are *representatives* of the complete Church. The term *angels* is still *symbolic* in John's interpretation. Students of God's Word and scholars alike have never come to a consensus in their interpretation of who the angels of Revelation 1:20 actually are. Some say they are heavenly beings. Others believe them to be human messengers, such as Church leaders. "Angel" might also stand for *every* true Gospel teacher who is enabled by God's Holy Spirit with authority to teach.

CHAPTER 6

Messages to Four Churches

Revelation 2

Ephesus (1)
1 Unto the angel of the church of Ephesus write; These things saith he that holdeth the seven stars in his right hand, who walketh in the midst of the seven golden candlesticks;
2 I know thy works, and thy labour, and thy patience, and how thou canst not bear them which are evil: and thou hast tried them which say they are apostles, and are not, and hast found them liars:
3 And hast borne, and hast patience, and for my name's sake hast laboured, and hast not fainted.
4 Nevertheless I have *somewhat* against thee, because thou hast left thy first love.
5 Remember therefore from whence thou art fallen, and repent, and do the first works; (**repeat**) or else I will come unto thee quickly, and will remove thy candlestick out of his place, except thou repent.

These are very sincere "religious" people, who have cooled off toward God to the point of being almost useless to the cause of Christ in the world. They have also cooled off in their love of *the brethren* who are the people of Christ's body. One cannot love God if there is no love for His body or His family. If you're a professing Christian and you find yourself repelled by religious people and institutions, and you won't even attempt to discern the genuine from the hypocrites, then ask God to put *His* love in your heart for *the brethren.* Seek to honor God by loving His people. Get involved with the *Church.*

History records Ephesus as being the most prominent modern and cultural seaport city in the Roman province of Asia. This city had a population of nearly a half million people. The church of Ephesus was birthed out of Pentecost, where the apostle Paul observed this *Holy Spirit event* with *Gentile Christians.* Ephesus had a strong Christian presence, but they were also steeped in other beliefs, including occultic practices and goddess worship. (Their patron god being the Greek fertility goddess, Diana.) Christians who did *not* worship Diana were shunned by the secular and religious leaders of Ephesus. John's message to the Christian church in Ephesus was to follow the one true God and to *forsake all idols.*

There were some genuine believers in the church of Ephesus, who recognized sin and idolatry in their church, and they hated it. God commended these genuine believers. However, over time, even these believers fell prey to the typical halfhearted and methodic observance of *religion.*

When we genuinely love Jesus Christ, we will love what He loves and hate what He hates. We will have a burden for bringing lost people to Christ. We will desire to be *fully* conformed to His character and mission. God's instruction to *this* church is: *"Remember, repent, and repeat* your first passion toward God or you will cease to exist as a Church. Your influence for the kingdom of God will be gone."

The image of Jesus holding the seven stars in his right hand (vs. 1) is a reminder to all Church *leaders* that it is *God* who holds them up. The Church *only* thrives because of the life-giving power of Jesus Christ and the light and fuel of the Holy Spirit.

6 But this thou hast, that thou hatest the deeds of the Nicolaitans, which I also hate.
7 He that hath an ear, let him hear what the Spirit saith unto the churches; To him that overcometh will I give to eat of the tree of life, which is in the midst of the paradise of God.

Even today, many *professed* "believers" among us are introducing God's people to damnable heresies and destructive policies. They are unfaithful to God's Word, mixing His truth with misinformation and outright lies.

> **2 Peter 2:1** But there were also false prophets among the people, even as there will be false teachers among you, who will secretly bring in destructive heresies, even denying the Lord who bought them…

The Nicolaitans were known for doing just this, under the guise of "liberty." They wanted the benefits of Christianity but also the perks, license, and lives of heretics and sinners. Their leaders preferred the *law* over *grace*, with its built-in control over the people.

The contemporary Church must be actively on guard against all such deception. Our best offense against *deception* is knowing

God's Word. We must recognize that there will be professed believers among us who prefer the sins of the world over the "narrow way." We must overcome evil, and stay *hot* for God and His truth.

Smyrna (2)

8 And unto the angel of the church in Smyrna write; These things saith the first and the last, which was dead, and is alive;

It is *Jesus* who is the first and the last, who was dead and is alive. Mark 9:31

9 I know thy works, and tribulation, and poverty, (but thou art rich) and *I know* the blasphemy of them which say they are Jews, and are not, but are the synagogue of Satan.

The very persecutors of the church of Smyrna were Jews by genetics and heritage. They believed that by *birthright* alone, they were the favored, chosen of God, yet they were actually hostile opponents of Christ. *God's eternal family will not be a genetically related family, but a spiritually related family.*

10 Fear none of those things which thou shalt suffer: behold, the devil shall cast *some* of you into prison, that ye may be tried; and ye shall have tribulation ten days: be thou faithful unto death, and I will give thee a crown of life.

The reference to *ten days* is to inform that the Church's tribulation trials will be for a *limited time* only, but John also informs that some trials may lead to martyrdom.

Smyrna, like Ephesus, was another large, modern, coastal trading center in Asia Minor. The government and citizens of Smyrna, primarily Jewish, were fully loyal to *Rome* and the Roman emperor. The Christian Church of Smyrna, however, suffered persecution because they chose loyalty to *Jesus* in the midst of a population that opposed Christianity.

Persecutions are often the means of trying and proving those who *profess* Christ. Afflictions reveal if one's faith and testimony for Jesus Christ is genuine. The faith of the church of Smyrna proved to be genuine, yet that was *not* a ticket for a life of no suffering and trials. That's not how it works.

Many people right now might *believe* that they have genuine faith, but should their stockpiles and back-up supplies and all earthly riches dry up, will their faith remain? When people have nothing left but their professed faith, their faith will either prove genuine or false. Pray that God will keep *you* and find *you* faithful. If you have *genuinely* accepted Jesus Christ as your Savior *and Lord*, God *will* be with you until the end. He *will* keep you. *You have the Holy Spirit to keep you faithful.*

Trials and tribulation not only confronted the church of Smyrna, but they *will* come to try and prove *our* faith as well. One day a "Man of Sin" will arrive on the scene and send out his workers with an iron-fisted message that no one can travel, get medical care, or purchase food unless they agree to take a *mandated mark of allegiance*, whatever that may be. Some believe that a needle may be the method of delivery for this "*mark*." I'm not really positive about what I believe regarding the mark of the beast; however, if I ever see a strong-armed, overstepping, coercive, powerful voice or entity *mandating* that *everyone* profess allegiance to a plan or action that *requires an identifier or a trackable mark or something injected into the body* (or else you will lose some of your God-given human rights), I would say, *without a doubt* you should *not* profess any allegiance or take *any* form of identifying *mark* of allegiance, nor *any* injection, to satisfy that entity! Don't let hunger in your belly win over your decision. Do *not* betray God. We know that *God will be faithful* to His children. We must trust God, even if we have to suffer greatly and perhaps die. Will you even hesitate? Think about this now. That day is approaching.

11 He that hath an ear, let him hear what the Spirit saith unto the churches; He that overcometh shall not be hurt of the second death.

There are communities of believers in our day, who like the Jews in Smyrna's day, feel they are God's only chosen people, based on faulty assumptions. These believers engage in *works of the Law and religious traditions* like the Jews in Smyrna, all while they reject the exclusive and effectual sacrifice of the Jewish Messiah, Jesus Christ, as the *only* means to cancel their sins and make them right with God. They view God as the Old Testament *Creator*, who is currently absent until He comes to their *future* promised rescue. They don't comprehend that God's rescue mission happened *on the Cross, and in His resurrection*, which was *one stage in his complete coming*. The redemption story continues until the *last day*, when the *last* enemy, death, is conquered. Some accept Christ's sacrifice *in part only* and cling to *heritage and works* to their own loss.

In the book of Romans, Paul differentiates *spiritual Jews* (true Jews) from those who can only claim a *genetic* connection to Abraham:

Romans 2:28–29 For no one is a Jew who is merely one out-wardly, nor is circumcision outward and physical. But a Jew is one inwardly, and circumcision is a matter of the heart, by the Spirit, not by the letter. His praise is not from man but from God.

Romans 2:6–11 instructs that God does *not* practice racial par-tiality. A *true Jew* is defined by God's holy Word.

Romans 2:6–11 He will render to each one according to his works: to those who by patience in well-doing seek for glory and honor and immortality, he will give eternal life; but for those who are self-seeking and do not obey the truth, but obey unrighteousness, there will be wrath and fury. There will be tribulation and distress for every human being who does evil, the Jew first and also the Greek, but glory and honor and peace for everyone who does good, the Jew first and also the Greek. For *God shows no partiality.*

Romans 17:26 And (God) hath made *of one blood* all nations of men for to dwell on all the face of the earth, and hath determined the times before appointed, and the bounds of their habitation;

The message from God to the Church of Smyrna is that there is no more condemnation to the *believers* who proclaim the divinity and lordship of Jesus Christ. Sin was judged at the Cross for *all* who overcome evil by their testimony of Jesus Christ and their faithfulness to Him. But there were Jews in this church who didn't understand this. Pride in their *heri-tage* and circumcision of the flesh (*works*) caused them to feel superior to the *spiritual Jews*, (*the redeemed Gentiles*) who were grafted into God's family by circumcision of the *heart* and *faith in Jesus Christ.*

Pergamos (3)

12 And to the angel of the church in Pergamos write; These things saith he which hath the sharp sword with two edges;

13 I know thy works, and where thou dwellest, *even* where Satan's seat *is*: and thou holdest fast my name, and hast not denied my faith, even in those days wherein Antipas *was* my faithful martyr, who was slain among you, where Satan dwelleth.

14 But I have a few things against thee, because thou hast there them that hold the doctrine of Balaam, who taught Balac to cast a stumbling block before the children of Israel, to eat things sacrificed unto idols, and to commit fornication.

15 So hast thou also them that hold the doctrine of the Nicolaitans, which thing I hate.

Pergamos was the two-century-long capital city and the Greek epicenter of culture in the Roman province of Asia. This city was a dangerous place to live for devout and dedicated followers of Jesus Christ. Pergamos boasted an educated population, a strong and sophisticated culture, pagan temples, and impressive buildings and architecture with many statues of the Greek gods and goddesses. These people worshipped pagan gods. It was a dangerous place for Christians to live *for God.* But even in this "seat of Satan," God rebukes their compromise with the ungodly world. Their compromises included idolatry, immorality, false teachings, and license to sin under the guise of liberty and grace. Under no circumstance are God's people excused to compromise with the world and live sinful lives.

16 Repent; or else I will come unto thee quickly, and will fight against them with the sword of my mouth.

The letter to Pergamos, while directed to *them*, encompasses *all* of the Church, and is a reference to *all* the oppression against God's people throughout history. God is speaking to *you and me* about compromise too.

Throughout history, certain "churches," or communities of believers, have mixed so much of the world into their affairs that they are represented by Pergamos. Pergamos is typified by these words: "where Satan dwells." John's vision of Jesus holding a sharp, two-edged sword depicts the Lord's readiness to bring severe judgment against Pergamos. Pergamos was *over-flowing* with religious and moral compromise. Like Pergamos, *today's* Christians are compromising their convictions, morals, and lifestyles for the sake of money, power, and personal gain. Pergamos Christians give no thought to the cost of sin, to our Savior. The lifestyle of Pergamos was primarily a consumption of the world's diet of pleasure and acquiring goods, with little time to commune with God and build *His* kingdom versus *their own*. Does that sound like us? Shudder!

The reference to Balaam and Balac in the church of Pergamos is an important reference. Balaam was solicited by a pagan king, Balac, to curse Israel. Balaam would not curse God's people because God told him not to. Balaam was a prophet who heard from God, but what he *really* wanted was the *carnal reward* King Balac offered to him. So, Balaam attempted to take a back-door route to gain his *earthly reward*. Instead of directly cursing Israel, Balaam taught King Balac that in order to overcome

Israel, he simply needed to entice them with sexual immorality and idolatry.

We have an abundance of church leaders and congregants today, who nudge the church to "lighten up and stop being so Old Testament!" They subtly introduce licentiousness and idolatry. *"Pray for your yacht, and mansion, and all the things the 'good-life' can offer. God wants you to be happy."* This is Pergamos.

17 He that hath an ear, let him hear what the Spirit saith unto the churches; To him that overcometh will I give to eat of the hidden manna, and will give him a white stone, and in the stone a new name written, which no man knoweth saving he that receiveth *it*.

In those days, the white stone had a significant meaning, which was understood by the people. When a person was on trial, the jury held two stones, a white one for an innocent verdict and a black stone for a guilty verdict. The jury used the stone to indicate to the judge if they found the person on trial to be innocent or guilty. God says that *overcomers* will be found innocent. The white stone meant the person would get a *clean slate*.

John's reference to the *hidden manna* is to remind the church where our provisions come from. God will never leave us nor forsake us. He will supply all of our needs, even by supernatural means if necessary.

Thyatira (4)
18 And unto the angel of the church in Thyatira write; These things saith the Son of God, who hath his eyes like unto a flame of fire, and his feet *are* like fine brass;

19 I know thy works, and charity, and service, and faith, and thy patience, and thy works; and the last to *be* more than the first.
20 Notwithstanding I have a few things against thee, because thou sufferest (allow) that woman Jezebel, (heresy and apostasy, toleration of false teachers) which calleth herself a prophetess, to teach and to seduce my servants to commit fornication, and to eat things sacrificed unto idols.
21 And I gave her space to repent of her fornication; and she repented not.
22 Behold, I will cast her into a bed, and them that commit adultery with her into great tribulation, except they repent of their deeds.

This is a bed of intense *suffering* that will be the demise of all who teach, encourage, or tolerate false doctrine, apostacy, and sin in the Church. The warning is also inclusive of all followers who *choose* to give their allegiance to apostate leaders. *Thousands of religious people, who expect to be included in God's eternal kingdom, sit under earthly leaders who blaspheme God with antichrist encyclicals, and unbiblical messages.* Those who *remain* in a covenant relationships with false teachers will continue to make excuses and remain on the membership rolls of adulterous churches. Unless they *come out from among them,* they will be cast into a bed of suffering.

23 And I will kill her children with death; and all the churches shall know that I am he which searcheth the reins and hearts: and I will give unto every one of you according to your works.

"Her children" are the converts she makes. They will not survive in the apostate atmosphere of this church. These misguided converts have a covenant relationship with their mother church, and will follow her, *despite awareness that their leadership brings in damnable heresies.*

24 But unto you I say, and unto the rest in Thyatira, as many as have not this doctrine, and which have not known the depths of Satan, as they speak; I will put upon you none other burden.
25 But that which ye have *already* **hold fast till I come.**
26 And he that overcometh, and keepeth my works unto the end, to him will I give power over the nations:
27 And he shall rule them with a rod of iron; as the vessels of a potter shall they be broken to shivers: even as I received of my Father.

God's faithful followers, the saints, are shepherded with His staff. In this millennium of time, right before the return of the Lord, we, the saints, will execute vengeance on the nations, per God's own decree.

> **Psalm 149:5-9** Let the saints be joyful in glory: let them sing aloud upon their beds. Let the high praises of God be in their mouth, and a two edged sword in their hand; To *execute vengeance upon the heathen*, and punishments upon the people; To bind their kings with chains, and their nobles with fetters of iron; To execute upon them the judgment written: *this honour have all his saints.* Praise ye the LORD.

> **Psalm 2:8-9** Ask of me, and I shall give thee the heathen for thine inheritance, and the uttermost parts of the earth for thy possession. *Thou shalt break them with a rod of iron;* thou shalt dash them in pieces like a potter's vessel.

28 And I will give him the morning star.

Christ will give *himself* to all those who *overcome*. He is the "Bright and Morning Star" in Revelation 22:16.

29 He that hath an ear, let him hear what the Spirit saith unto the churches.

Thyatira was a prosperous trading town of simple folk. Small businesses and trading unions were their notoriety. They sold and traded leather, purple-colored dyes, pottery, cloth, and food, among other things. Every artisan was a member of a trading guild. Their trading guilds, or unions, were quite powerful and dictated expectations to the community. The artisans were required to sacrifice to the patron gods of the whatever goods they sold or traded. Their meetings were lewd and lascivious, with sexual encounters with prostitutes. Failure to participate meant being ostracized by the leaders and community and most likely losing one's livelihood.

So Thyatira did what the popular culture did. Eventually, the church of Thyatira exuded the immoral spirit of Jezebel and was full of idolatry and sin. There were still *some* God-fearing people in this church, mainly because they had strong *roots*. In their *beginning*, they demonstrated a strong faith, affirming their love for God by genuinely serving Him and caring for others.

Idolatry is commonly practiced in modern churches, world-wide. It is seen in the worship and veneration of icons and relics, statues, and saints, and "celebrity" human leaders. Some churches even idolize their music teams and musicians. But often, those who are *most* idolatrous in our contemporary churches, idolize *themselves* and their possessions.

Although Thyatira's body of professed believers have many attributes of faithfulness, there are those in this Church who *choose to follow* "Jezebel" into compromise, which always leads to inevitable *deception*. If "Jezebel" ever raises her whorish head in *your* church, cast her out.

This reference to Jezebel in this Church is *metaphorical* of the sexually immoral, idolatrous, false prophetess, Jezebel, of the Old Testament, where we read of her *followers* who also engaged in her sins. The warning from God to this congregation of believers is, once again: *repent.* "*I will cast her on a bed of suffering, and I will make those who commit adultery with her suffer intensely, unless they repent of her ways. I will strike her children dead*" (Rev. 2:22–23).

Sobering.

CHAPTER 7

Messages to Three Churches

Revelation 3

Sardis (5)

1 And unto the angel of the church in Sardis write; These things saith he that hath the seven Spirits of God, and the seven stars; I know thy works, that thou hast a name that thou livest, and art dead.
2 Be watchful, and strengthen the things which remain, that are ready to die: for I have not found thy works perfect before God.

Sardis had at one time been a most important city of Asia Minor. Its wealth primarily came from mineral resources, the wool industry, and the manufacture of textiles. Through several devastating circumstances, this very prosperous and secure city crumbled. They were conquered in hostile Persian invasions and devastated by major earthquakes. Their once secure, vibrant, and economically sound city was now frail and indefensible. They rebuilt a new, strong-looking city that appeared very secure from future invasions. It is *this* new vibrant city of Sardis that John addresses.

This church of Sardis *appears* to onlookers as a hospitable and vibrant place. That is their reputation. They had a name, or a reputation, in the world (to the earth-dwellers), *but that isn't what God saw.* God saw a *dead* church.

So, what is the message to *this* church? "*I have not found thy works* perfect *before God.*" What? It is certain that *none* of man's works are *perfect* before God. *Jesus Christ,* alone, is *the perfect* and only begotten of God. To get the deeper meaning of God's message through John, think about the story of Cain and Abel. Cain's sacrifice was not acceptable because it was through his *own* efforts that he thought he could please God. Abel, through spiritual understanding, sacrificed the firstling of his flock as a reverential and worshipful offering to God. Cain, on the other hand, brought to God a gift consisting of what *he* accomplished (works). His gift was *self*-admiring. Man cannot please God with their *self*-efforts, or "works." *Faith* in the perfect atoning work of Jesus Christ, *apart from all self-efforts,* is what is *required* to please God. This church lacks *genuine* faith. They attempt to commend themselves to God, bringing their own efforts, not completely trusting *His* effectual sacrifice.

3 Remember therefore how thou hast received and heard, and hold fast, and repent. If therefore thou shalt not watch, I will come on thee as a thief, and thou shalt not know what hour I will come upon thee. 4 Thou hast a few names even in Sardis which have not defiled their garments; and they shall walk with me in white: for they are worthy. 5 He that overcometh, the same shall be clothed in white raiment; and I will not blot out his name out of the book of life, but I will confess his name before my Father, and before his angels. 6 He that hath an ear, let him hear what the Spirit saith unto the churches.

The church of Sardis is representative of some of our contemporary churches, as well as this first-century church. The professed believers in the church of Sardis are the *spiritually dead congregants* of the very body they profess to be a part of. They may even ritually pray daily (to their "Santa Claus" God,) seeking to get the "stuff" they want in life: health, money, favor, and peace. They never really seek to *know* this God that they petition so frequently.

Sardis performs service for the church or community when asked. That is a good thing. In the Epistle of James, the brother of Jesus declares, "Faith, if it hath not works, is dead." Nevertheless, Sardis performs *dead* works before God because they consider their *own* efforts as *meritorious* in their *justification* with God. *All* of our justification with God is *imputed.* Christ *in* us is our righteousness. Faith unites us to Christ, *apart from our performance.*

Sardis rarely desires to hear or read God's holy Word *in private communion* with God. They lack *personal* communion with God and *personal* relationship with him because they don't really have *genuine* faith in the full gospel of God. That is why they are "dead." *Everything else* is more important than this "moral" book, the Bible. They see God's Word as a collection of interesting stories to keep people on the moral high ground. They do *not* understand the Word as being God's personal and individual message *for them* and all people. They are the walking dead, meaning they are not connected to the True Vine, *and they don't even know it.*

But don't forget, Sardis was never accused of immorality, idolatry, greed, legalism, or witchcraft. Nevertheless, they were "*dead*" because they lost their *zeal* for God and were *just religious*. We need to also search our own hearts and see if we have fallen into this trap. Strengthen what remains. Wake up. Overcome. Read the Word of God. Grow in faith.

<u>Philadelphia</u> (6)

7 And to the angel of the church in Philadelphia write; These things saith he that is holy, he that is true, he that hath the key of David, he that openeth, and no man shutteth; and shutteth, and no man openeth;

8 I know thy works: behold, I have set before thee an open door, and no man can shut it: for thou hast a little strength, and hast kept my word, and hast not denied my name.

9 Behold, I will make them of the synagogue of Satan, which say they are Jews, and are not, but do lie; behold, I will make them to come and worship before thy feet, and to know that I have loved thee.

Philadelphia was a city named in honor of the love their founder had for a brother. This city of "brotherly love," was an early seat of Christianity. It was located in Asia Minor and was populated by many Jews. The population was somewhat transient, as many people would leave the city after earthquakes, which happened rather frequently, as they were located on a fault line.

Jesus encourages the Church of Philadelphia by acknowledging that that their persecutors are religious hypocritical liars, who will one day witness and acknowledge that God loves them. Jesus exhorts the church of Philadelphia to overcome evil by remaining faithful to him in the face of the many, inevitable trials which they face in their pagan culture. These words are to encourage *the entire body of Christ* to remain faithful. *We* live in quite a pagan culture in this day and age as well. We *also* need to overcome evil by remaining faithful to God. It is *God* who empowers the Church to share the Gospel. *He* is the one who opens and closes doors and hearts. Just answer His call, and He has a place to send *you* to be His witness.

The hostile, Jewish opposition to this faithful church, Philadelphia, is met with brotherly love so unfamiliar to them. The Jews, despite being in possession of holy writ, had *no love* for Jesus Christ. But, as a result of this Church's *bold* witnessing and brotherly love, one day, the *national* Jews will acknowledge God's blessing on the loving Church of Philadelphia.

For many centuries, the unredeemed, lost, and blind, Christ-rejecting Jewish people have claimed to be God's *only* true children, the children of Abraham. But scripture points to a *New Jerusalem,* which is Jesus Christ's family by *spiritual* birth. The *spiritual* Jews are *both redeemed Jews and Gentile Christians* in God's chosen family. The *true* children of Abraham are not carnal, Christ-rejectors, even if they are the *most* religious Jewish people and are living in Israel. *Faith in Jesus Christ,* not mere nationality, determine *true* Judaism.

10 Because thou hast kept the word of my patience, I also will keep thee from the hour of temptation, which shall come upon all the world, to try them that dwell upon the earth.

Once again, earth-dwellers are those who oppose God. They are *the unrighteous.*

Only the saints of God, have *citizenship in heaven* and will be kept from "the hour of temptation," *the seven last plagues,* which deliver God's wrath on the *ungodly.*

Those who keep the gospel in a time of peace, shall be kept by Christ in an hour of temptation; and the same Divine grace that has made them fruitful in times of peace, will make them faithful in times of persecution.[3]

11 Behold, I come quickly: hold that fast which thou hast, that no man take thy crown.

The word *hast* is a past-tense verb. It does *not* say, 'Hold fast to a *new* revelation.' God's *written* Word is all we need to hold fast to.

12 Him that overcometh will I make a pillar in the temple of my God, and he shall go no more out: and I will write upon him the name of my God, and the name of the city of my God, *which is* new Jerusalem, which cometh down out of heaven from my God: and *I will write upon him* my new name.
13 He that hath an ear, let him hear what the Spirit saith unto the churches.

Laodiceans (7)
14 And unto the angel of the church of the Laodiceans write; These things saith the Amen, the faithful and true witness, the beginning of the creation of God;
15 I know thy works, that thou art neither cold nor hot: I would thou wert cold or hot.
16 So then because thou art lukewarm, and neither cold nor hot, I will spue thee out of my mouth.
17 Because thou sayest, I am rich, and increased with goods, and have need of nothing; and knowest not that thou art wretched, and miserable, and poor, and blind, and naked:
18 I counsel thee to buy of me gold tried in the fire, that thou mayest be rich; and white raiment, that thou mayest be clothed, and *that* the

shame of thy nakedness do not appear; and anoint thine eyes with eye salve, that thou mayest see.

19 As many as I love, I rebuke and chasten: be zealous therefore, and REPENT.

20 Behold, I stand at the door, and knock: if any man hear my voice, and open the door, I will come in to him, and will sup with him, and he with me.

21 To him that overcometh will I grant to sit with me in my throne, even as I also overcame, and am set down with my Father in his throne.

22 He that hath an ear, let him hear what the Spirit saith unto the churches.

The church of Laodicea is illustrative of *the final apostate church*, which has *nothing to commend*. This church really has nothing to do with the *true* Savior, the Son of God, the image of the invisible, eternal, Omnipotent *God in Christ Jesus*. John's vision of this apostate church presents a community of believers who are wretched, *self-deceived, spiritually bankrupt*, and pitiful, all while believing that they are rich and blessed. These are spiritually blind, self-righteous, religious hypocrites who *don't even recognize their condition* nor their need. While they are nominally "Christian," Christ has no position of authority in their congregation or lives.

These people might be in our family, or be our neighbors, or co-workers, who may even engage in a little "God talk" at times. They feel "Christian enough" if they simply avoid getting into disagreements with staunch lovers of truth or defenders of the faith. They desire to be "saved," but they don't really want to seek, serve, and obey God. They are on death's doorstep spiritually, and they are *mightily deceived*. John's message to them, from God, is to repent, and to overcome their deceitful desires and practices that choke out the Word of Truth. They need to stop being lukewarm and apathetic, and take note of their true condition.

This Church scares me. They are in the *worst* spiritual condition of all the seven churches John wrote letters to, but they think they are the favored bride of Christ. They think they have God in their back pocket. They have enough of everything, so they boast of being *favored* and *blessed* by God. They may have beautiful church buildings and programs that are the envy of community organizations. But in reality, they are *not* God-made; they are *self*-made. They are prideful, lukewarm, self-sufficient, self-centered, wretched, pitiful, poor, blind, and naked to God. They really need God for *nothing* to do what they are doing. They use His name (in vain) to build *their* church. Frightening to think about.

We have come to the end of the letters to the seven churches. So we see, God knows the efforts, challenges, and trials of *every* believer, in *every* church, in *every* age. The entire Bible is God's story and shows how God relates to mankind, what He requires of us, and what He offers to us.

Revelation's theme is repentance. The message to the Church is that the Church must remain faithful *until the end.* Although the circumstances, influences, and difficulties vary in every community or congregation of believers and in every individual life, God wants it clearly understood that He knows what is going on, and that *His body (the Church) must overcome evil by their faithfulness to Him* so that they can receive a future reward and eternal salvation. Note that John did *not* write letters to the *worldly,* outside of the Church. They are the earth-dwellers who are the eternally lost, hell-bound souls, who will face God's fury, and eternal separation from all that is good, *unless* they come to God through *obedience* and *by His calling*.

From this point on, following chapters 1–3, many sincere Christians believe that the rest of the chapters in the book of Revelation are written specifically, and exclusively, to the *Jews*. They believe that "the Church" will be raptured out of the world *before* the apocalyptic events in the upcoming chapters. Little applies to *them* after chapter 3, according to them. Their basis for this belief is their claim that there is no direct reference to "the Church" beyond this point. But that is *not* true. There are direct references to "the saints" on earth, who are an obvious reference to "the Church" which is the body of Christ.

Whenever we read of "the saints" in Revelation, we *are* reading about the Church. The people of God, or the Church, of *every* kindred, nation, tongue, and people is surely visible throughout the following chapters in the book of Revelation. Nothing suggests that the "saints" in these chapters are only Jews, or a *select group* of end-time tribulation saints, as some claim. There is *not* a separate group of saints who are *not* a part of the Church. *There is but one body of Christ.*

Scripture informs that the Church *of every age* enters the kingdom of God *through much tribulation:*

> **Acts 14:22** Confirming the souls of the disciples, and exhorting them to continue in the faith, and that we must through much tribulation enter into the kingdom of God.

Some pretribulationists believe that God has a special place in His heart for 'His favored bride,' who they feel to be a *select* company of end-time saints, including themselves, who will be *exempt* from suffering tribulation at the end of time. This teaching is unscriptural. In the book of Acts, the first century Church was *birthed* into tribulation. Persecution against God's people *is* tribulation to the ones enduring it. God is no respecter of persons. In what century in biblical text does the Church have immunity from tribulation and suffering? None.

> **Acts 3:1–3** And Saul approved of their killing him. (Stephen) On that day a great persecution broke out against the church in Jerusalem, and all except the apostles were scattered throughout Judea and Samaria. Godly men buried Stephen and mourned deeply for him. But Saul began to destroy the church. Going from house to house, he dragged off both men and women and put them in prison.

God always seeks His rightful place among His body of believers. He promises rewards and eternal benefit to those who heed and obey His words. He promises punishment and destruction to those who refuse to repent. God desires to prevent judgment that will befall all sinners who refuse His corrections. He has mercifully warned and corrected sinners since the beginning of creation. God's discipline and judgment is meant for unbelievers and hypocrites, and the *un*faithful who will *not* heed correction and be rescued. His *final judgments* will be highlighted in the concluding chapters of Revelation. They are severe, and ultimately eternal, *for those who refuse to repent.*

CHAPTER 8

Wow, God!

Revelation 4

1 After this I looked, and, behold, a door *was* opened in heaven: and the first voice which I heard *was* as it were of a trumpet talking with me; which said, Come up hither, and I will shew thee things which must be hereafter.

2 And immediately I was in the spirit: and, behold, a throne was set in heaven, and *one* sat on the throne.

3 And he that sat was to look upon like a jasper and a sardine stone: and *there was* a rainbow round about the throne, in sight like unto an emerald.

4 And round about the throne *were* four and twenty seats: and upon the seats I saw four and twenty elders sitting, clothed in white raiment; and they had on their heads crowns of gold.

The twenty-four elders are a figurative depiction of representatives of both the Gentile Church and the redeemed Jews. Here you have the triune God on His throne in heaven, surrounded by His complete Church—from the Old Testament times (twelve tribes) to the New Testament times (twelve apostles).

5 And out of the throne proceeded lightnings and thunderings and voices: and *there were* seven lamps of fire burning before the throne, which are the seven Spirits of God.
6 And before the throne *there was* a sea of glass like unto crystal: and in the midst of the throne, and round about the throne, *were* four beasts full of eyes before and behind.

The four beasts are representative of all living creatures.

7 And the first beast *was* like a lion, and the second beast like a calf, and the third beast had a face as a man, and the fourth beast *was* like a flying eagle.

John's vision of the *four beasts* is connected with the appearances described in Isaiah 6:2 and Ezekiel 1:10. These angelic beings are called *seraphim* in Isaiah and *cherubim* in Ezekiel. Ezekiel sees *four living creatures*, each with *four faces*: that of a *man*, a *lion*, an *ox*, and an *eagle* (Ezek. 1:10). The cherubim and seraphim, and are always pictured as the devoted servants of God and the workers of His purposes and judgments.

In the Old Testament, in Genesis 3:24, we see the cherubim at the entrance of the garden of Eden. In Psalm 80:1, the Shepherd of Israel dwells between the cherubim on His mercy seat. Ezekiel 41:18 says the dwelling-place of God is adorned with cherubim. The seraphim, or "fiery ones," are seen in God's divine presence (Isa. 6:2). They have the appearance of "living beings," symbolizing all created life. These *representatives in heaven* are the swift workers of God's will. They are one of the manifestations of God's profound glory and unrivaled power.

The four beasts in Revelation 4:6–7 are represented as: (1) a creature like a *lion*, representative of *wild animals*; (2) a creature like a *calf or an ox*, representative of *domestic animals*; (3) a creature with *a human face*, representative of *mankind*; and (4) a creature like an *eagle*, representative of all *flying creatures.*

Together, these four beasts are symbolical of *God's entire creation*, fulfilling His will in their proper roles to ultimately bring forth God's glory. The human-faced beast is *not* a picture of the Church because *the Church is separately represented by the twenty-four elders.* The human faced beast is a picture of *unredeemed* mankind.

8 And the four beasts had each of them six wings about *him*; and *they were* full of eyes within: and they rest not day and night, saying, Holy, holy, holy, Lord God Almighty, which was, and is, and is to come.

These representatives of *all created life* sing "*Holy, holy, holy*" to the triune Godhead: the Father, Son, and Holy Ghost. They sing Holy, holy, holy to the Everlasting God which **is**, which *was*, and *which is to come,* the Almighty (Rev. 1:8). Living creatures throughout the earth and the intermediate heaven *never stop* singing praises to God. Try this. If you have a smart phone, put your video app on slo-mo and record the evening insects when they are loudly making their creature noises. Then listen to the recording. They are singing amazing songs of praise.

9 And when those beasts give glory and honour and thanks to him that sat on the throne, who liveth for ever and ever,
10 The four and twenty elders fall down before him that sat on the throne, and worship him that liveth for ever and ever, and cast their crowns before the throne, saying,

11 Thou art worthy, O Lord, to receive glory and honour and power: for thou hast created all things, and for thy pleasure they are and were created.

Again, it is important to reinforce that the book of Revelation is not a chronologically ordered presentation of events, nor a chronological "story." This fourth chapter might actually be a vision of the very *end* of the Apocalypse, when every knee bows before the Son of God and confesses Him as Lord.

The whole of Revelation includes:

1. *John's letters* to the seven churches;
2. John's visions of *seal and trumpet judgments;*
3. *Interludes* with more details about the time of these judgments;
4. *The last day*—The cataclysmic, great day of the Lord, with the gathering of all the saints, (the "rapture"). This is the New Jerusalem (Christ's bride) descending from heaven and the simultaneous outpouring of God's wrath on all of the unrepentant, God-hating rebels on earth. That "day" includes the final battle, Armageddon; and
5. *Restoration*: A new heaven and new earth descends from heaven.

There are some final declarations of blessings and warnings in the last chapter.

At the conclusion of Revelation, God's eternal purpose and the mystery of God are fulfilled and complete. God has gathered a devoted people for Himself, and He will live with them in eternity, where rebellion will *never* arise again.

Also, let it be noted before we progress forward, there's not a single scripture in the book of Revelation, or anywhere else in the Bible, that says or even suggests that *everything* in the book of Revelation happens *only* during a seven-year period, or during "*the* seven-year tribulation" at the very end of time.

CHAPTER 9

A *Real* History Book!

Revelation 5

1 And I saw in the right hand of him that sat on the throne a book written within and on the backside, sealed with seven seals.

> **Ezekiel 2:9-10**And when I looked, behold, an hand *was* sent unto me; and, lo, a roll of a book *was* therein; And he spread it before me; and it *was* written within and without: and *there was* written therein lamentations, and mourning, and woe.

This scroll, with the *seven* seals, represents *all* the history of humanity since creation, along with the mysteries of God. This is the scroll of Ezekiel 2:9, with lamentations and mourning and woe. This scroll book is full and complete, with writing on both sides, and guarded with seven seals. The contents, although never read by John nor fully revealed, are *symbolically* depicted by what progressively takes place as each seal is opened. Although John is witnessing the opening of the seven seals in succession, God operates outside of time and space. That means that the events do not necessarily happen progressively, or sequentially, in our sense of time. The events are a symbolic vision given to John to see the *condition* of the Church and the world at the end of time.

The *mysteries of God* and the kingdom of heaven could only be understood by Jesus and to whom He revealed them, while He was on earth. Jesus gave his disciples a *partial revelation,* but He said the mysteries of the kingdom of heaven could *not* be understood by the multitudes (earth dwellers).

> **Matthew 13:10-11** And the disciples came, and said unto him, Why speakest thou unto them in parables? He answered and said unto them, Because it is given unto you to know the mysteries of the kingdom of heaven, but to them it is not given.

After telling his disciples that He would let them in on "the mysteries," here is what Jesus said to His followers.

> **Matthew 13:24-30** Another parable put he forth unto them, saying, The kingdom of heaven is likened unto a man which sowed good seed in his field: But while men slept, his enemy came and sowed tares among the wheat, and went his way. But when the blade was sprung up, and brought forth fruit, then appeared the tares also. So the servants of the householder came and said unto him, Sir, didst not thou sow good seed in thy field? from whence then hath it tares? He said unto them, An enemy hath done this. The servants said unto him, Wilt thou then that we go and gather them up? But he said, Nay; lest while ye gather up the tares, ye root up also the wheat with them. Let both grow together until the harvest: and in the time of harvest I will say to the reapers, Gather

ye together first the tares, and bind them in bundles to burn
them: but gather the wheat into my barn.

Matthew 13:47-49 Again, the kingdom of heaven is like unto
a net, that was cast into the sea, and gathered of every kind:
Which, when it was full, they drew to shore, and sat down,
and gathered the good into vessels, but cast the bad away. So
shall it be at the end of the world: the angels shall come forth,
and sever the wicked from among the just,

**2 And I saw a strong angel proclaiming with a loud voice, Who is
worthy to open the book, and to loose the seals thereof?
3 And no man in heaven, nor in earth, neither under the earth, was
able to open the book, neither to look thereon.
4 And I wept much, because no man was found worthy to open and
to read the book, neither to look thereon.
5 And one of the elders saith unto me, Weep not: behold, the Lion of
the tribe of Juda, the Root of David, hath prevailed to open the book,
and to loose the seven seals thereof.**

The sealed scroll and the seals *magnify who the Lamb is—the
worthy Son of God*. The Lion of the tribe of Judah, the offspring
of David is none other than *Jesus Christ*.

**6 And I beheld, and, lo, in the midst of the throne and of the four
beasts, and in the midst of the elders, stood a Lamb as it had been
slain, having seven horns and seven eyes, which are the seven Spirits
of God sent forth into all the earth.**

Remember, *the elders* are a figurative depiction of the twenty-four representatives of the complete Church—both the

redeemed Gentiles, the twelve tribes of Israel, and the redeemed Jews, the twelve apostles.

> **Ephesians 2:19–20** So then you are no longer strangers and aliens, but you are fellow citizens with the saints and members of the household of God, built on the foundation_ of the apostles and prophets, Christ Jesus himself being the cornerstone,

> **Revelation 21:12** And had a wall great and high, and had twelve gates, and at the gates twelve angels, and names written thereon, which are the names of the twelve tribes of the children of Israel:

> **Revelation21:14** And the wall of the city had twelve foundations, and in them the names of the twelve apostles of the Lamb.

The elders told John to look at a Lion, but what John saw when he looked was *a Lamb*. The *Lamb* represents *Jesus Christ*. The *seven horns* represent God's complete omnipotent *power*. The *seven eyes* represent God's omniscience. This is a picture of the *Holy Spirit* in the *seven Spirits of God* (Rev. 1:4).

> **Revelation 4:5** And out of the throne proceeded lightnings and thunderings and voices: and *there were* seven lamps of fire burning before the throne, which are the seven Spirits of God.

The seven lamps of fire burning before the throne indicates that the Holy Spirit is an *illuminator*. He makes the things of God clearer to the one in whom He dwells. Unredeemed human beings are in a state of *darkness. This is a moral darkness, not intellectual.* The unredeemed man *cannot* know the things of God. *They may investigate the literal words of the Bible, but they have no ability, apart from the indwelling of the Holy Spirit, to comprehend the truths of God.*

The *four beasts* represent *all living creatures.* This is a vision of Jesus Christ, the worthy Lamb of God, in the midst of the throne of God and in the midst of *the representatives of all His creation.*

7 And he came and took the book out of the right hand of him that sat upon the throne.
8 And when he had taken the book, the four beasts and four *and* twenty elders fell down before the Lamb, having every one of them harps, and golden vials full of odours, which are the prayers of saints.

The prayers of the saints are preserved and are never ineffectual to God. Our prayers matter to Him. They can also move metaphorical mountains. So pray.

9 And they sung a new song, saying, Thou art worthy to take the book, and to open the seals thereof: for thou wast slain, and hast redeemed us to God by thy blood out of every kindred, and tongue, and people, and nation;
10 And hast made us unto our God kings and priests: and we shall reign on the earth.
11 And I beheld, and I heard the voice of many angels round about the throne and the beasts and the elders: and the number of them was ten thousand times ten thousand, and thousands of thousands;
12 Saying with a loud voice, Worthy is the Lamb that was slain to receive power, and riches, and wisdom, and strength, and honour, and glory, and blessing.

13 And every creature which is in heaven, and on the earth, and under the earth, and such as are in the sea, and all that are in them, heard I saying, Blessing, and honour, and glory, and power, *be* unto him that sitteth upon the throne, and unto the Lamb for ever and ever.

Verses 8 and 13 reveal that every creature God has ever created commemorates their redemption by praising and adoring Him and singing a new song—*a song of the redeemed* (Rev. 5:13).

14 And the four beasts said, Amen. And the four *and* twenty elders fell down and worshipped him that liveth for ever and ever.

Again, the twenty-four elders are a *figurative depiction* of the representatives of both the Gentile Church and the redeemed Jews: twelve tribes of Israel and twelve apostles.

CHAPTER 10

Redemptive Seals 1–5 and then the End—Seal 6.

Revelation 6

Seal 1

1 And I saw when the Lamb opened one of the seals, and I heard, as it were the noise of thunder, one of the four beasts saying, Come and see. 2 And I saw, and behold a white horse: and he that sat on him had a bow; and a crown was given unto him: and he went forth conquering, and to conquer.

This vision comes from the first beast of the four living creatures in Revelation 4:7, which is the lion. Jesus Christ is known as the *Lion of the Tribe of Judah.* This is the conquest of the gospel. This is a prophecy of victory. Nothing in Seal 1 is said about blood, war, or deception. *Conquering* is for the purpose of *overcoming. Overcoming and conquering* has been *God's purpose* for the Church since its birth. The Church is fulfilling God's ultimate purpose: to conquer evil and gather for Himself a devoted people to eternally dwell with.

The man on the white horse is wearing a victor's crown, or a diadem, which is a *royal* crown. He has an instrument of war. Loud voices of heavenly beings, or thunder, will often accompany divine pronouncements and actions, as it does in verse 1 above.

> **Revelation 3:21** The one who *conquers,* I will grant him to sit with me on my throne, *as I also conquered* and sat down with my Father on his throne. ESV

> **John 16:33** I have told you these things so that in me you may have peace. You will have suffering in this world. Be courageous. I have *conquered* the world. Christian Standard Bible

> **Romans 8:37** No, in all these things *we are* more than *conquerors* through Him who loved us. ESV

> **Romans 12:21** Do not be *conquered* by evil, but *conquer evil* with good. ESV

> **Zechariah 1:8–10** I saw by night, and behold, a man riding on a red horse, and it stood among the myrtle trees in the hollow; and behind him were *horses: red, sorrel,* and *white.* Then I said, "My lord, what are these?" So the angel who talked with me said to me, "I will show you what they are." And *the man* who stood among the myrtle trees answered and said, "These are the ones whom the LORD has sent to walk to and fro throughout the earth. Berean Study Bible

The opening of the first seal is John's vision of the triumphant Christ and His Church. The white horse is symbolic that this mission to conquer is *righteous* and is *from heaven.* The whole message of this first seal is to understand right off the bat that Christ and the Church *will* prevail. Jesus Christ *has overcome* the world and will ultimately and finally put down all rebellion forever. The Church will share the victory with Christ Triumphant. The first seal's message is meant *to comfort and encourage* God's people that we *will* come through this time of tribulation with victory. By Christ's victory on the Cross, and His resurrection, we who believe on Him and stay loyal to Him *to the end* will triumph, conquer, and overcome. The Holy Spirit is given to God's people, to give us all the strength we need to stay loyal to Christ. We are not orphans here.

This appearance of the rider on the white horse is later repeated (with additions) in Revelation 19:11. As previously noted, John re-references earlier visions, in order to progressively *reveal* details. The introduction of a vision does *not* denote its happening in a *linear* fashion or on a chronological timeline. Compare the events in Revelation to an author expounding on a moment in time, detail-by-detail, paragraph-after-paragraph, until the whole situation can be properly understood in all its facets.

Christ and His kingdom will finally and ultimately conquer evil during the Apocalypse. All earthly empires are going down. Mankind's empires are only temporary. It is only *Christ's* kingdom which has no end. Until the kingdoms of this world are conquered, there will continue to be strife between the powers of earth and the powers of heaven. Christ and His Church *will* conquer—finally and completely. That will be the complete and final act of God in our redemption.

Seal 2

3 And when he had opened the second seal, I heard the second beast say, Come and see.

4 And there went out another horse *that was* red: and *power* was given to him that sat thereon to take peace from the earth, and that they should kill one another: and there was given unto him a great sword.

This vision allowed John to witness the results of a world-wide war, including the persecution and martyrdom of the *saints* for Christ. This vision comes from *the second beast*, the calf or ox, animals that are also symbolical of sacrifice and death. The great sword represents a sacrificial knife and persecution. With God's full knowledge and permission, Christians, the saints, the very redeemed of God, have been severely persecuted and martyred over all the centuries, working out *God's ultimate plan to conquer evil*. This taking peace from the earth is not necessarily one particular time of war, at the end of time only. Jesus said, "I came *not* to send peace, but a *sword*" (Matt. 10:34). Seal 2 represents what has been ongoing on the earth ever since Cain murdered Abel at the beginning of this temporal world.

It is *God's kingdom*, the New Jerusalem, that will usher in a heavenly government ruled by Jesus Christ. *Peace will never come by human efforts. Peace will come when God's kingdom comes and His will is done.*

Seal 3

5 And when he had opened the third seal, I heard the third beast say, Come and see. And I beheld, and lo a black horse; and he that sat on him had a pair of balances in his hand.

6 And I heard a voice in the midst of the four beasts say, A measure of wheat for a penny, and three measures of barley for a penny; and *see* **thou hurt not the oil and the wine.**

This voice comes from the midst of the four beasts, who are the representatives of all creation. The vision depicts great scarcity, but not the complete absence of provisions. The voice prohibits the rider on the black horse from hurting the oil and the wine, signifying that there is still a means of grace and mercy.

The sword, pestilence, and famine are often seen in scripture as expressions of God's fierce anger. The scarcity John sees in this third-seal vision may include events that have already happened *prior* to our lifetime, *and* that are happening *in* our lifetime, as well. Scarcity in the world has occurred over the ages, and will continue to recur until the end of the world. This affliction surely happens concurrently with John's other visions. The judgment of famine on earth is also not necessarily representative of *one* particular time at the end of days.

Seal 4
7 And when he had opened the fourth seal, I heard the voice of the fourth beast say, Come and see.
8 And I looked, and behold a pale horse: and his name that sat on him was Death, and Hell followed with him. And power was given unto them over the fourth part of the earth, to kill with sword, and with hunger, and with death, and with the beasts of the earth.

This livid-colored horse depicts terror, disease, and death. It perhaps describes the color of persons affected by a plague. The very name of the rider that sat on this pale horse was *Death*. Hell followed him to claim his victims. *Hell* always follows the death of the unredeemed. The devil will claim his eternal victims, those who have rejected the lordship of Jesus Christ. Isaiah writes of the connection between death and hell: "*Hell from beneath is moved for thee to meet thee at thy coming*" (Isa. 14:9).

Revelation also makes the connection of *death and hell.* They *always* go hand in hand for the lost. We read of *"the keys of hell and of death"* in Revelation 1:18, and *"Death and hell delivered up the dead"* in Revelation 20:13, 14.

"Over the fourth part of the earth" suggests that a *portion* of *all* mankind must be afflicted with sword, with hunger, and with the beasts, which can be wild animals and/or pestilence. Even a deadly world-wide virus could account for a portion of the large-scale death count. John sees that the number killed is not a small number, but certainly is less than half of the population. *"One fourth"* is a symbolic quantity. Throughout the course of life, Christians are not exempt from death, but Christians are *never* under the authority of Satan. God has *bound* Satan from exercising *authority* over *His people.* Christians can petition God in faith, and God *will* act on our behalf when we ask according to His will—in faith. Read 1 John 5:14, 15.

The Old Testament prophet, Ezekiel saw into the future. Ezekiel 14:21 highlights "four sore judgments": the *sword, famine,* the *noisome beast,* and the *pestilence.* Pain, and suffering in all its forms are represented by these judgments.

John's vision in Revelation 6 also pertains to the persecution and tribulation of the body of Christ *in every age.* Even today, Christians are persecuted and murdered around the world daily because of their testimony and profession of faith in Jesus Christ.

In the first century, Christians were thrown to lions for sport in pagan amphitheaters. They died by the wild beasts of the earth.

Ezekiel's four sore judgments are related to the opening of the first four seals, where the land, sea, fresh springs of water, and the sky are being destroyed as permitted by God to afflict *all* mankind. Afflictions allow mankind to see the goodness, the severity, and the mercy of God. They are permitted by our Father God's chastening hand. It is intended that when sorrow and distress come to a man, he should call on God and experience His comfort and mercy. If we lived luxurious, peril-free lives, absent of all afflictions, you can be certain that we would *not* call on God to our own eternal detriment.

God's judgments often happen simultaneously and are ongoing. Figuring out the *time periods* of the judgments is *not* the message we need to take away from these visions. Instead, we must consider that Christians of *every* age must remain faithful, among the unholy, unrighteous, enemies of God, in times of plenty and in times of scarcity. We must endure and be faithful *until the end* in this lost and dying world.

In Matthew 24:7, 13, Jesus foretold, *"Nation shall rise against nation, and kingdom against kingdom; and there shall be famines, and pestilences, and earthquakes, in divers places."* We are seeing all this today. Actually, that verse sounds like a current newspaper headline.

The worldwide COVID-19 plandemic (Yes, I meant to say "plandemic"), at the time of this writing, is rapidly making inroads in toppling economies, breaking the food chain, creating the possibility of a worldwide famine, creating a new "unity for a cause" between the world's leaders, and setting the stage for a world government and world religion. Under the pretense of the welfare of its citizens, unregenerated government leaders, along with powerful billionaires, are posing as benevolent overseers and setting the stage to legislate totalitarian policies and mandated reforms over the entire population of mankind, including churches. They have already politicized the COVID-19 virus to dictate where and how Christian congregants can and cannot assemble to practice their faith and worship of God in public spaces. These changes happened almost overnight.

There is now a call for a worldwide, required, implanted/injected "mark," or a *vaccine*, rumored to come *with a digital ID* and/or papers of government approval, to "save and protect" mankind. It has been suggested in the mainstream media that this vaccine should be tied to human rights and commerce, or buying and selling, transportation, employment, and health care. Sounds like a sinister allegiance to the Man of Sin, or to his antichrist system to me.

This COVID-19 plandemic has launched the perfect entryway for professional propaganda hucksters, liars, and change agents to manipulate the masses. Their lies and propaganda are *psychological warfare*, but few people are even aware. *Propaganda* is a systematic effort to persuade a body of people to support or adopt a particular attitude or course of action. It is typically circulated through the mass media and is based on distortions, half-truths, outright lies, and *fear*. It is *always* connected with fear. Satan is behind all manipulative, deceptive propaganda and policy that attempts to unify the masses to restructure under a central administration "for their own good." When the citizens of a nation have been properly conditioned through *fear*, they can more easily be *conquered*. And our citizens are being conditioned and conquered even without the use of force. Satan is very cunning and deceptive. People are ready to relinquish their historical, natural human rights to become cooperative citizens *of the world* (earth-dwellers.) "for the greater good of all." Wow. How did we get here so suddenly?

While we all sit by and watch what is happening in the rapidly changing world, I asked God, "What will the Revelation "tribulation period" really look like? How will we recognize that we are in *the very last days* just prior to the second coming of Christ?" God spoke to my heart and said, "*It will look just like this. The time of tribulation will look like the people and events you see right now in the world today, but the judgments and suffering will intensify greatly and will be more frequent and local for all.*"

Wow. We have all been waiting for beasts and scorpions, water full of dead animals, falling celestial bodies, multi-headed monsters, microchips, guillotines, and swarms of locusts, when the picture *right in front of us* is the inception and intensification of last days tribulation. Tribulation started when the Church was born. *Seven years of tribulation is the complete amount of time throughout all history, in which Christ and his complete Church conquer the complete enemy for all eternity.* The seven years of tribulation is a symbolic period of time. It is a time within the symbolic "thousand years." The *seals* are the *ongoing redemptive methods* of God to make people yearn for a better place and to bring them *to repentance.* The *trumpet judgments* are God's *punishments* to convince men to fear God and turn to Him in *repentance* because He has the power to cast them into the eternal flames of the devil's hell. The *bowl or vial judgments* are God's *wrath* against the stubborn, unrepentant earth-dwellers who cannot be redeemed. These judgments are not for God's people.

Seal 5

9 And when he had opened the fifth seal, I saw under the altar the souls of them that were slain for the word of God, and for the testimony which they held:

A believer's testimony is *the active showing forth of genuine Christian faith*, not only by words, but by deeds. One's lifestyle of words *and* deeds are what display genuine faith in Jesus Christ's life and work.

In verse 9, John calls the martyrs "souls" because they don't have their glorified bodies yet. *Glorified bodies are given to the saints at the day of the dead* (when saints' graves open up) during the simultaneous rapture. The saints aren't raptured until the *last trumpet on the last day.*

Is there any biblical history of God allowing his servants to go through trials of faith? Yes there is. God's faithful followers, throughout the decades, have suffered afflictions, tribulation, and persecutions, with God's full knowledge and consent. "*I came not to send peace, but a sword*" (Matt. 10:34).

Martyrs are those who yield up their lives for God. The bodies of the martyrs will be glorified and reunited with their souls on the last day. Where the *souls* are, scripture says that they are *at rest* (Rev. 6:11) and in peace, yet remain in full expectation of the final conclusion of this age, where all the saints, in glorified bodies, will come into the presence of God and dwell with Him forever. The souls of those who are slain for Christ, *during every age* of tribulation, are *waiting* to descend with Christ from heaven at the last day.

10 And they cried with a loud voice, saying, How long, O Lord, holy and true, dost thou not judge and avenge our blood on them that dwell on the earth?

In our daily lives, God's people may not always easily recognize those who are earth-dwellers because many can fool **us** with their *exteriors of pretense*. We cannot see their hearts, like God does. However, we can often learn about creatures by observing their appetites. Observe people's "appetites." Do you see any real hunger for the things of God in the people you observe?

Earth-dwellers (even religious people who identify as "Christian") primarily spend their lives seeking the *world's* goods, pleasures, and accolades. They may even call their earthly treasures "God's riches" or "blessings." But the riches and pleasures of the earth are seductive. They lead to the sin of pride, which then produces a desire for recognition and *prestige*. People who are caught up in seeking power, fame, prestige, money, influence, recognition, worldly wisdom, luxuries, and delicacies may be *totally sin-sick*, and *unaware*. Many are seeking to rule their own lives so they can glory in their success. So many visibly, successful, professing "Christian" people are watching stock market tickers *more* than they are watching for opportunities to serve God *and* more than they are watching for the return of the omnipotent King of kings.

Other earth-dwellers seek sexual exploits and independence from biblical morals and constraints. Their deceived, carnal hearts believe that God just wants them to have a good time and enjoy life and all its pleasures. To anyone who is a *genuine* follower of Jesus Christ, these earth-dwellers easily and more *obviously* appear as sin-sick rebels against God. Sadly, we have people in Christian churches who fall into this category and are also unaware of their state.

11 And white robes were given unto every one of them; and it was said unto them, that they should rest yet for a little season, until their fellow servants also and their brethren, that should be killed as they *were*, should be fulfilled.

For a "little time," or "a little season," means *until the second coming of Christ.* This "little time" comes to an end and merges into eternity *at the seventh trumpet.*

Seal 6 The *Last Day* of this Age
12 And I beheld when he had opened the sixth seal, and, lo, there was a great earthquake; and the sun became black as sackcloth of hair, and the moon became as blood;

This is the same earthquake that we see in Revelation 16:18.

13 And the stars of heaven fell unto the earth, even as a fig tree casteth her untimely figs, when she is shaken of a mighty wind.
14 And the heaven departed as a scroll when it is rolled together; and every mountain and island were moved out of their places.

When the sky rolls up, the stars fall, and every mountain and continent on the earth is moved out of its place, it is *the end,* folks. *The sixth seal is clearly the end of this age, or the end of this world,* yet this is *early* in the book of Revelation. That's okay. The events in Revelation are *revealed* in the order God chose.

This sixth seal is a description of God judging and avenging those who have persecuted the Church *throughout all the ages* and in response to the souls who asked, *"How long?"* in Revelation 6:10.

The end of the world is also described by the prophet Isaiah. Isaiah 34:4 is a *parallel* of the events described in Revelation 6:13–14.

> **Isaiah 34:4** And all the host of heaven shall be dissolved, and the heavens shall be rolled together as a scroll: and all their host shall fall down, as the leaf falleth off from the vine, and as a falling fig from the fig tree.

15 And the kings of the earth, and the great men, and the rich men, and the chief captains, and the mighty men, and every bondman, and every free man, hid themselves in the dens and in the rocks of the mountains;
16 And said to the mountains and rocks, Fall on us, and hide us from the face of him that sitteth on the throne, and from the wrath of the Lamb:
17 For the great day of his wrath is come; and who shall be able to stand?

I don't believe that the point we are to take away from this allegorical passage about men hiding in dens and rocks of the mountains is to figure out where these mountains are. They are *not* literal. John's allegorical writing represents *spiritual* truths through concrete or material forms. The Apocalypse is not a literal story.

Revelation, chapter 7, is where we will find the answer to the question in 6:17, "*Who shall be able to stand?*" The answer is, *the sealed of God.*

Revelation 7 is a *parenthetical interlude* for John to add and explain details, *which he now sees* but that are related to an *earlier* vision. These judgments in his visions *overlap* with others. *We know the seals and trumpet judgments overlap because the sixth seal and seventh trumpet culminate on the same day.*

It is in chapter 7 where we read of John's vision of *a great, numberless multitude of all nations, kindreds, peoples, and languages,* who are *the sealed* of God and who come *out of* great tribulation.

Chapter 8 adds *more details* about the *other judgments during this same time.* The additional details in this chapter are the trumpet judgments. They happen in concert, or simultaneously, at the time of the seal judgments, particularly toward the end of the seals as the day of the Lord draws near. When we get to the end of seal six, we are also at trumpet seven. This reveals that trumpets 1–6 have been happening in unison with seal judgments. We are at the *end* of this age. The world will be burned up and recreated by God. *The rapture occurs at the seventh trumpet, which is also at the sixth seal.* The seventh seal simply depicts the handing over of the seven trumpets to the seven angels. The symbolic number seven simply lets us know that all *this is coming from God.* God started the trumpet judgments *before* John *saw* the vision of the trumpets coming from God. Put your chronological, time-line bias away. I know; it's hard.

After the resurrection of Jesus Christ, the *resurrection* of *all* who belong to Christ is the *next* resurrection on the agenda (1 Cor.

15:23). Scripture says *that resurrection day* occurs *after* the tribulation *of those days.* There is no separate, **secret** rapture. *There is only the one rapture in conjunction with this resurrection of the dead in Christ.*

The *entire* Bible is not presented in sequential or chronological order. When we read the Old Testament, we notice that events in one time period and chapter are written about in later books and chapters. These are the same stories and time periods but with new details. In Revelation, John *retells* about periods of time, again and again, with new details as well.

On the last day, when the sixth seal is opened and the seventh angel sounds, the redeemed body of Christ is *raptured* to meet the Lord in the air, with the dead in Christ. That day is the great and dreadful day of the Lord. That is the day when the New Jerusalem (Christ's bride) descends from heaven with Jesus Christ. All the armies of God and all the redeemed of every age rise up to meet with Jesus in the air. At that time, all of God's chosen people will get glorified, eternal bodies. *The saints are not on earth for God's wrath.* But now it starts. The *bowl judgments* immediately follow the rescue of God's people, and the wrath of God is delivered on all the unrighteous rebels on earth.

In Matthew 24, we see Jesus speaking *to the Jews,* describing the Revelation judgments (The Olivet Discourse). We also read of these apocalyptic judgments in Mark 13 and Luke 21, written *to the Gentiles.* These judgments that Jesus describes are the seals and the trumpets, and also contain some details from the Old Testament prophets. Jesus was describing *the conclusion* of this present age. Even as a man, Jesus had full knowledge of the Old Testament scriptures.

In the Old Testament, various prophets described events that would lead up to the return of the Lord. A number of Old Testament prophets wrote about, "that day," or "*the day of the Lord.*" They called the *last day*, "the day of the Lord's anger" and "the day of the Lord's vengeance." The events leading up to that day are called "a time of great distress" or "a time of tribulation" and are described as "a time when God's wrath will come upon the earth." According to Daniel's prophecies, this distress happens during a period of "seventy weeks of years." Jesus knew all of these prophecies. But he doesn't use *our* calendars and clocks. *Apocalyptic numbers and time quantities are figurative and symbolic.* Jesus often taught using *spiritual symbolism.*

Some would like to claim that that Matthew 24 (the Olivet Discourse) applies only to the genetic Jews and is not relevant to the Church. They make this claim because Jesus's last major discourse was spoken to a Jewish audience. But Mark 13 and Luke 21 also contain the Olivet Discourse, and these Gospels were written with a *Gentile* audience in mind. When Jesus gave his final discourse about His coming at the end of the world, He spoke to a Jewish audience because these were *His followers.* In other words, those who followed Him and believed His message were the invisible Church, His *spiritual* body—the *true* Jews.

While some claim that Matthew 24 has no relevance to *the Church,* these same persons believe that the rapture, found *in the same discourse,* is meant for *the Church,* and therefore for them. All of the Olivet Discourse is for all of the Church indeed.

Jesus describes the *end* of this age (the Olivet Discourse).

Matthew 24:3–22

3 And as he sat upon the mount of Olives, the disciples came unto him privately, saying, Tell us, when shall these things be? and what shall be the sign of thy coming, and of the end of the world?

4 And Jesus answered and said unto them, Take heed that no man deceive you.

5 For many shall come in my name, saying, I am Christ; and shall deceive many.

6 And ye shall hear of wars and rumours of wars: see that ye be not troubled: for all these things must come to pass, but the end is not yet.

7 For nation shall rise against nation, and kingdom against kingdom: and there shall be famines, and pestilences, (deadly viruses) and earthquakes, in divers places.

8 All these are the beginning of sorrows.

9 Then shall they deliver <u>you</u> up to be afflicted, and shall kill you: and ye shall be hated of all nations for my name's sake.

10 And then shall many be offended, and shall betray one another, and shall hate one another.

11 And many false prophets shall rise, and shall deceive many.

12 And because iniquity shall abound, the love of many shall wax cold.

13 But he that shall endure unto the end, the same shall be saved.

14 And this gospel of the kingdom shall be preached in all the world for a witness unto all nations; and then shall the end come.

15 When ye therefore shall see the abomination of desolation, spoken of by Daniel the prophet, stand in the holy place, (whoso readeth, let him understand:)

16 Then let them which be in Judaea flee into the mountains:

17 Let him which is on the housetop not come down to take any thing out of his house:

18 Neither let him which is in the field return back to take his clothes.

19 And woe unto them that are with child, and to them that give suck in those days.

20 But pray ye that your flight be not in the winter, neither on the sabbath day:

21 For then shall be great tribulation, such as was not since the beginning of the world to this time, no, nor ever shall be.

22 And except those days should be shortened, there should no flesh be saved: but for the elect's sake those days shall be shortened.

Jesus describes the sixth seal/seventh trumpet:

Matthew 24:29–31

29 Immediately *after* the tribulation *of those days* shall the sun be darkened, and the moon shall not give her light, and the stars shall fall from heaven, and the powers of the heavens shall be shaken:

30 And *then* (after the tribulation) shall appear the sign of the Son of man in heaven: and then shall all the tribes of the earth mourn, and they shall see *the Son of man coming* in the clouds of heaven with power and great glory.

31 And he shall send his angels with a great sound of a trumpet, *and they shall gather together his elect* from the four winds, from one end of heaven to the other.

This is the *same description* of the sixth seal (the *end*) in Revelation 6:12–15. Revelation 16:17–21 gives *more details* about the same thing. *The sixth seal and the seventh trumpet are one event.* The seventh seal launches John's *vision* of the simultaneous and parallel trumpet judgments. At the seventh trumpet, the saints are caught up to be with the Lord, and *at the same time, out of the seventh trumpet comes the seven bowl judgments and the wrath of God.* Again, when we read about God's *wrath* in Revelation, we are reading about the *end.* God's wrath is not poured out until the end, when the Church is safely out of the way. There are *not* numerous and different times that God pours out His wrath.

Now we are going to read the *parenthetical passage,* Revelation 7. In Revelation 7, John reveals the *fact* that both Jews and Gentiles will be saved and rewarded *as one body.*

The seven seals are not limited to an exclusive last literal seven years, that we call, "*the* tribulation." The seals are symbolic and depict God's ongoing avenging and judgment of his opponents in the fallen world *in every age.*

Read the Old Testament to see the numerous times God delivered penalties and judgments on the prideful and powerful *rebels* in the world. Read Leviticus 26:14–39, and you will see trouble on every side, drought, famine, poverty, disaster, sword, pestilence, disease, persecution, and defeat *waged by God* against the disobedient. This tribulation of God's judgments is a *part* of the *vertical deliverance* of the seal and trumpet judgments. These judgments come *from above* and have been coming from God since the fall of man. They are punitive and yet *redemptive*, and they *will* increase in frequency and intensity at the end of this age.

Satan is actually on a "leash" all the time. He is *bound* from having *full* reign. During this symbolic thousand-year millennium, Satan *cannot* overcome a man's freewill. He *can* deceive, accuse, and tempt, and bring harm and evil into the earth, but he does *not* have the power of death. Satan has been cast out of the heavenlies and is *bound*. That does *not* mean that he cannot operate here on earth. He has a *great degree* of *destructive powers*, allowed by God. When the second coming of Christ is imminent, however, Satan will *not* be on God's "leash." *He will be loosed for a short time.*

CHAPTER 11

The Complete Church Sealed

Revelation 7

1 And after these things I saw four angels standing on the four corners of the earth, holding the four winds of the earth, that the wind should not blow on the earth, nor on the sea, nor on any tree.

2 And I saw another angel ascending from the east, having the seal of the living God: and he cried with a loud voice to the four angels, to whom it was given to hurt the earth and the sea,

3 Saying, Hurt not the earth, neither the sea, nor the trees, till we have sealed the servants of our God in their foreheads.

This is symbolic. God already knows who belongs to Him, and He doesn't need a physical mark on our foreheads to find us.

> **2 Cor. 1:21-22** Now he which stablisheth us with you in Christ, and hath anointed us, is God; *Who hath also sealed us*, and given the earnest of the Spirit in our hearts.

> **Rev. 22:4** And they shall see his face; and his name shall be *in their foreheads*.

4 And I heard the number of them which were sealed: *and there were* sealed an hundred *and* forty *and* four thousand of all the tribes of the children of Israel.

5 Of the tribe of Juda *were* sealed twelve thousand. Of the tribe of Reuben *were* sealed twelve thousand. Of the tribe of Gad *were* sealed twelve thousand.

6 Of the tribe of Aser *were* sealed twelve thousand. Of the tribe of Nepthalim *were* sealed twelve thousand. Of the tribe of Manasses *were* sealed twelve thousand.

7 Of the tribe of Simeon *were* sealed twelve thousand. Of the tribe of Levi *were* sealed twelve thousand. Of the tribe of Issachar *were* sealed twelve thousand.

8 Of the tribe of Zabulon *were* sealed twelve thousand. Of the tribe of Joseph *were* sealed twelve thousand. Of the tribe of Benjamin *were* sealed twelve thousand.

9 After this I beheld, and, lo, a great multitude, which no man could number, of ALL nations, and kindreds, and people, and tongues, stood before the throne, and before the Lamb, clothed with white robes, and palms in their hands;

What John *heard* and what he *saw* were not exactly the same. But remember, God directed John to write what he *saw*. In verse 9, John wrote about what he *beheld*, or what he **saw**. John saw a revelation of God's eternal kingdom, the new heaven and new earth, made up of *all* the redeemed of the Lord. He *saw* the Old Testament believers and the New Testament believers, *together*, who make up *spiritual Israel*, or the Church. The 144,000 children of Israel in verse 6:4 are *all of Abraham's spiritual children.*

In verse 4 John *heard* of the sealing of the whole house of *redeemed Israel*, but this is what John *saw*: Then he beheld, or *saw*, a *great multitude of all nations, and kindreds, and people, and tongues.* The number 144,000 is a symbolic number. Many want to insist that this number is literal, yet they are able to understand that the candlestick is symbolic, the four corners of the earth is symbolic, the Lamb is symbolic, the sword in his mouth is symbolic, the door and the keys are symbolic, the anointing of the eyes with a salve is symbolic, the measure of wheat for a penny is symbolic, the colored horses are symbolic, the white stone is symbolic, the beast from the sea is symbolic, Sodom and Egypt are symbolic, the beasts and the little book are symbolic, the whore of Babylon is symbolic, and almost everything in Revelation is symbolic, or figurative.

This great multitude coming from all nations, languages, and people is a picture the complete Church. It is *not* a simple depiction of national Israel and the original twelve tribes. This symbolic number encompasses both Old and New Testament redeemed representatives. The *spiritual tribes* of Israel are joined into *one body* with the *redeemed Gentiles.* Those who believe in Jesus as the Christ are *spiritual Israel.*

> **Rom. 9:6b-7** For they are not all Israel, which are of Israel: 7 Neither, because they are the seed of Abraham, are they all children: but, In Isaac shall thy seed be called.

> **Rom. 9:8** That is, They which are the children of the flesh, these are not the children of God: but the children of the promise are counted for the seed.

> **Gal. 3:26–29** For ye are all the children of God by faith in Christ Jesus. For as many of you as have been baptized into Christ have put on Christ. There is neither Jew nor Greek, there is neither bond nor free, there is neither male

nor female: for ye are all one in Christ Jesus. And if ye *be* Christ's, then are ye Abraham's seed, and heirs according to the promise.

Notice that the tribes of Israel named in verses 5–8 do *not* include Dan and Ephraim. They, instead, include Joseph, who was not one of the twelve tribes. What is the significance of that?

This depicts that *there is no "national salvation" for any group of people.* When John wrote about what he heard and what he saw, he intended to show that God's plan is *not* about *national* Israel. *All who will be saved by Jesus Christ will be saved the same way: by their acceptance of the complete and effectual atoning sacrifice of Jesus Christ on the Cross, plus nothing else.* The throne of God is *not* accessible to sinners. Both Jews and Gentiles who *reject* God's grace will be lost and cast into the devil's hell for all eternity. There is not a separate gospel and grace for different national groups. The *only* access to God and His gift of salvation is through Jesus Christ and His by grace alone. *No one will go to heaven based on nationality.* Anyone attempting to get to heaven *another way* is a thief and a robber, according to God's Word. They will *not* gain entrance.

> **John 10:1** Verily, verily, I say unto you, He that entereth not by the door into the sheepfold, but climbeth up some other way, the same is a thief and a robber.

> **John 10:7** Then said Jesus unto them again, Verily, verily, I say unto you, I am the door of the sheep.

Of the symbolic 144,000, scripture says, "*These are they which were not defiled with women; for they are virgins*" (Rev. 14:4).

Just as the number 144,000 is symbolic, so is this statement about their being *virgins*. Are we to believe that this verse is talking about 144,000 males who have not committed sexual sin with women? No. That's pure nonsense. The 144,000 are *not* a gender-specific group of men with a claim to fame of being male virgins.

This large company of believers are *all* those who have proved themselves *faithful to God*. They have suffered persecution in order to *voluntarily separate* themselves from the world while *in* the world. These are witnesses who are *not* a part of the harlot system. *They have spiritually removed themselves from the mind-set of Babylon, the whore.*

10 And cried with a loud voice, saying, Salvation to our God which sitteth upon the throne, and unto the Lamb.
11 And all the angels stood round about the throne, and *about* the elders and the four beasts, and fell before the throne on their faces, and worshipped God,
12 Saying, Amen: Blessing, and glory, and wisdom, and thanksgiving, and honour, and power, and might, *be* unto our God for ever and ever. Amen.
13 And one of the elders answered, saying unto me, What are these which are arrayed in white robes? and whence came they?

White robes are the garment of priests. We, the Church, are priests to God.

> **Revelation 5:10** And hast made us unto our God kings and priests: and we shall reign on the earth.

14 And I said unto him, Sir, thou knowest. And he said to me, These are they which came out of great tribulation, and have washed their robes, and made them white in the blood of the Lamb.

Revelation 7:14 does *not* say, "*were kept from great tribulation,*" but "*came out of*" it. "*Washed their robes*" is symbolic of *obedience* to God's commandments, and living by *faith* in all that God says in His Word.

15 Therefore are they before the throne of God, and serve him day and night in his temple: and he that sitteth on the throne shall dwell among them.
16 They shall hunger no more, neither thirst any more; neither shall the sun light on them, nor any heat.
17 For the Lamb which is in the midst of the throne shall feed them, and shall lead them unto living fountains of waters: and God shall wipe away all tears from their eyes.

CHAPTER 12

Pass the Trumpets and Start the Judgments.

Revelation 8

Seal 7

The seventh seal is opened, but it serves as a *transition*, not a judgment.

1 And when he had opened the seventh seal, there was silence in heaven about the space of half an hour.

The seventh seal is a segue, a transition made without pause or interruption to the seven trumpets. Seals 1–6 have been opened and *may* still be ongoing. *Seal six is the end.* The sky rolls up and the stars fall. *The sixth and seventh seal happen in conjunction with the seventh trumpet.* They are parallel and simultaneous. At the time of these judgments, God Himself gives seven angels the seven trumpets. The passive voice in Revelation typically shows an action *of/from God,* as does the number seven. (i.e., *"to them were given"*) Picture the judgments coming *down* together, rather than sequential events. Picture them *falling.*

Trumpets 1–6 were *already* falling *with* the first five seals, probably being delivered *closer to the time of the second coming,* and now the seventh and last trumpet judgment is coming down from God, in concert, with the sixth seal.

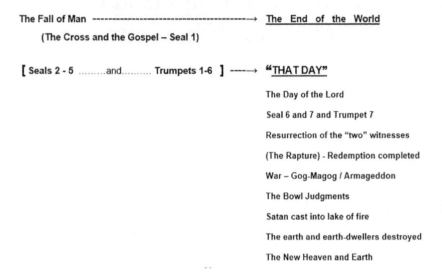

God's Complete Redemptive Plan

The Fall of Man --------------------------------------→ The End of the World
  (The Cross and the Gospel – Seal 1)

[Seals 2 - 5 ....and.......... Trumpets 1-6] ----→ **"THAT DAY"**

The Day of the Lord

Seal 6 and 7 and Trumpet 7

Resurrection of the "two" witnesses

(The Rapture) - Redemption completed

War – Gog-Magog / Armageddon

The Bowl Judgments

Satan cast into lake of fire

The earth and earth-dwellers destroyed

The New Heaven and Earth

Notice how much of Revelation is about *that day*—that one figurative day.

2 And I saw the seven angels which stood before God; and to them were given seven trumpets.

In this vision, the angels are *preparing to sound,* but we won't read about *the seventh trumpet* until Revelation 11:15. The visions are not about the *order* in which distinct judgments will happen, but are about *what* happens.

Revelation 8 is not the chapter where the seventh trumpet sounds, even though all seven angels are handed trumpets in this chapter. The first four trumpets are sounded in Revelation 8:6–13. Chapter 9 describes the fifth and sixth trumpets, which are the first two *woes*. Before John's vision of the seventh trumpet sounding, he inserts an *interlude,* where he *adds details and information* about *what else he saw* occurring *during the seals and trumpets.* Chapters 10 and 11 are interludes. The typologies and symbols in these flashback chapters are not easily understood, so don't get discouraged. I don't believe that the *point* of every symbol in Revelation is for us to figure out a literal meaning. The point is the *spiritual* application.

3 And another angel came and stood at the altar, having a golden censer; and there was given unto him much incense, that he should offer *it* **with the prayers of all saints upon the golden altar which was before the throne.**
4 And the smoke of the incense, *which came* **with the prayers of the saints, ascended up before God out of the angel's hand.**

Our prayers to God are *not* ineffectual. They are handled by *angels* and presented to God. Keep praying whether you see what is happening by the hand of God on your behalf or not. Prayer does move mountains.

5 And the angel took the censer, and filled it with fire of the altar, and cast *it* **into the earth: and there were voices, and thunderings, and lightnings, and an earthquake.**

This is a vision of the *beginning* of God's wrath, but the actual wrath occurs *at* the seventh trumpet. *This all happens very quickly.*

6 And the seven angels which had the seven trumpets prepared themselves to sound.

During the opening of the sixth seal, the ongoing six trumpet judgments will also culminate *very quickly* and will roll right into the seventh seal and seventh trumpet, *which is when the rapture occurs and the day of God's wrath begins.*

The first five seals in John's *recursive vision* happen over a period of time *throughout history.* In the end of time, as the day of the Lord approaches, these redemptive, corrective, and punitive seal judgments are overlapping, and toward the end, occur parallel to the first six *trumpet* judgments. These *combined judgments* are just the beginning of God's unbridled anger that will occur on *the day of the Lord.* The sixth seal and the seventh trumpet *immediately* precede the *wrath* of God on all those who have *refused* to repent and receive God's *numerous opportunities* for His grace and rescue.

Trumpet 1 *(These trumpet judgments, to some degree, may also happen throughout the course of time, but we will definitely see an increase and intensification of them near the very end.)*

7 The first angel sounded, and there followed hail and fire mingled with blood, and they were cast upon the earth: and the third part of trees was burnt up, and all green grass was burnt up.

Trumpet 2

8 And the second angel sounded, and as it were a great mountain burning with fire was cast into the sea: and the third part of the sea became blood;
9 And the third part of the creatures which were in the sea, and had life, died; and the third part of the ships were destroyed.

Trumpet 3

10 And the third angel sounded, and there fell a great star from heaven, burning as it were a lamp, and it fell upon the third part of the rivers, and upon the fountains of waters;
11 And the name of the star is called Wormwood: and the third part of the waters became wormwood; and many men died of the waters, because they were made bitter.

Trumpet 4

12 And the fourth angel sounded, and the third part of the sun was smitten, and the third part of the moon, and the third part of the stars; so as the third part of them was darkened, and the day shone not for a third part of it, and the night likewise.

> **Joel 2:10-11** The earth shall quake before them; the heavens shall tremble: the sun and the moon shall be **dark**, and the stars shall withdraw their shining: And the LORD shall utter his voice before his army: for his camp is very great: for he is strong that executeth his word: for the day of the Lord is great and very terrible; and who can abide it?

The Three Woes Are Pronounced

13 And I beheld, and heard an angel flying through the midst of heaven, saying with a loud voice, Woe, woe, woe, to the inhabiters of the earth by reason of the other voices of the trumpet of the three angels, which are yet to sound.

John's vision of the three woes pronounced by an angel against the earth-dwellers happens *during* the time of the last three trumpets, (5, 6, 7), and that would also be *during the seal judgments*. John *announces* these woes during this interlude we are in so he can fill in more details before he writes *about* the bowl judgments that come with the sounding of the seventh trumpet.

In the interludes of Revelation 10 and 11, John *gives details about* trumpet judgments 5 and 6. These judgments are ongoing, right into the sixth seal, which is the end of time on earth. When John writes about the sixth seal, the great day of God's wrath, he is also telling about the judgments of the seventh trumpet that simultaneously happens with seal 6 (Rev. 6:17; 11:15–19).

The "third part," repeated *numerous* times in verses 8:7 through 8:12, is symbolic, signifying a considerable number—more than a quarter but less than half.

CHAPTER 13

Demons, Death, and Destruction

***

Revelation 9

Trumpet 5

1 And the fifth angel sounded, and I saw a star fall from heaven unto the earth: and to him was given the key of the bottomless pit.

(From the heavenly realms.)

2 And he opened the bottomless pit; and there arose a smoke out of the pit, as the smoke of a great furnace; and the sun and the air were darkened by reason of the smoke of the pit.

John refers to this falling star as "him" and "he." This is imagery of a mighty ruler who comes to earth and is allowed to open up a destructive pit full of tormentors and demons. The key is symbolic.

> **Luke 10:18** And he said to them, "I saw Satan fall like lightning from heaven."

> **Revelation 12:9** And the great dragon was thrown down, the serpent of old who is called the devil and Satan, who deceives the whole world; he was thrown down to the earth, and his angels were thrown down with him.

The Old Testament story of Job shows on a small scale, what is going on with the whole human race during the time of Revelation 9. *God's people* have a *hedge* around them *unless God allows access* through the hedge. Satan is actually *bound* from destroying God's children. In the story of Job, God *did* allow the destructive powers of Satan access to Job, for his own omniscient reasons. God gave the "keys" of the hedge to Satan to "prove" Job. He was *not* allowed to take his life.

> **Job 1:12** And the LORD said unto Satan, Behold, all that he hath is in thy power; only upon himself put not forth thine hand. So Satan went forth from the presence of the LORD.

The scenario depicted in Revelation 9:1 is the same scenario we see in Job, the main difference being that the scale of Satan's destructive power is *global* in the end. *God still assigns the extent of Satan's power and reach.*

Satan was once a holy angel in heaven, but was cast out, for leading a rebellion against God. (Luke 10:18). He became the "prince of *this* world." However, when Jesus was lifted up on the Cross, Satan lost his kingdom (John 12:31–32).

Satan was cast out of the heavenlies to the realms of this world, but God did *not* give him any *authority* over *the Church*. God gave the saints, his faithful followers, *power* to "tread on serpents and scorpions, and power over *all* the power of the enemy"

(Luke 10:19). Jesus said that evil spirits are *subject* to *the Church* (Luke 10:20).

It sure doesn't appear that Satan is *not* fully operational here on earth. It looks like he's running the whole show. Nevertheless, he is currently *bound* on behalf of *God's* people. His wicked operations surely do affect *everyone* on earth. But he will be cast into the lake of fire at the end of the world.

**3 And there came out of the smoke locusts upon the earth: and unto them was given power, as the scorpions of the earth have power.
4 And it was commanded them that they should not hurt the grass of the earth, neither any green thing, neither any tree; but only those men which have not the seal of God in their foreheads.** *(the earth-dwellers)*

The passive voice, "*it was commanded*" is used because *God* gives the command that the wicked (locusts) *cannot* hurt His children, *the saints.* Praise the Lord for that!

Again, this sealing is symbolic. God has *already* sealed his people with the Holy Spirit, and He *knows* who are His. When we are saved, we are sealed. We were even *chosen* before the foundation of the world.

> **Revelation 7:3** Saying, Hurt not the earth, neither the sea, nor the trees, till we have sealed the servants of our God in their foreheads.

These "servants of God" are God's elect, chosen people—the *spiritual* Church on earth. God *will* make adequate provisions for the Church in the time of the end. He is faithful.

Ephesians 1:12–13 That we should be to the praise of his glory, who first trusted in Christ. In whom ye also trusted, after that ye heard the word of truth, the gospel of your salvation: in whom also after that ye believed, ye were sealed with that holy Spirit of promise,

John 6:27 Labour not for the meat which perisheth, but for that meat which endureth unto everlasting life, which the Son of man shall give unto you: for him hath God the Father sealed.

2 Timothy 2:19 Nevertheless the foundation of God standeth sure, having this seal, The Lord knoweth them that are his. And, Let every one that nameth the name of Christ depart from iniquity.

2 Corinthians 1:22 Who hath also sealed us, and given the earnest of the Spirit in our hearts.

Revelation 22:4 And they shall see his face; and his name shall be in their foreheads.

God's rich and effectual grace will preserve the saints from the final and complete apostasy that envelops the whole world in the very last days. *We are not to fear; God has the ability to manage these affairs and meet all of our needs.* We must always obey God without consideration of the consequences.

5 And to them it *was* given that they should not kill them, *(the earth-dwellers)* but that they should be tormented five months: and their torment *was* as the torment of a scorpion, when he striketh a man.

The tormentors are obviously some kind of demonic beings.

Five months equals a limited time. That's all we know. This is a symbolic time.

6 And in those days shall men seek death, and shall not find it; and shall desire to die, and death shall flee from them.

These men who want to die and can't are wicked earth-dwellers. Nothing they have ever trusted to deliver them from pain and suffering will work now. No drugs, no money, no alcohol, no weapon, no power and prestige—*nothing*. This is a judgment sent from God Almighty.

7 And the shapes of the locusts *were* like unto horses prepared unto battle; and on their heads *were* as it were crowns like gold, and their faces *were* as the faces of men.
8 And they had hair as the hair of women, and their teeth were as *the teeth* of lions.
9 And they had breastplates, as it were breastplates of iron; and the sound of their wings *was* as the sound of chariots of many horses running to battle.
10 And they had tails like unto scorpions, and there were stings in their tails: and their power *was* to hurt men five months.

These are frightening and very scary looking creatures, most certainly not natural beings of our animal kingdoms. These are not bugs that eat plants. They are not man-made war devices either. These figurative locusts with scorpion stings are *demonic creatures* loosed on earth by God, for the judgment of the wicked. These demons are minions of the devil, and they will hunt down and hurt every single person who is not sealed by

God. They will hurt them *painfully*, for a long, but limited time. They are murderous demons who were locked up in the pit until this time.

11 And they had a king over them, *which is* the angel of the bottomless pit, whose name in the Hebrew tongue *is* Abaddon, but in the Greek tongue hath *his* name Apollyon.

The bottomless pit is another name for the *abyss*. This is Satan's address, where his operations are conducted on earth. The bottomless pit is also the dwelling place of demons and the unsaved dead. This is hades. It is a penal place of confinement for all those awaiting judgment. The bottomless pit is under God's control. This is not the same as the lake of fire, or eternal hell.

John gives two forms of Satan's name, in Greek and Hebrew. These names sum up his character as a *murderer* and *destroyer*.

12 One woe is past; *and*, behold, there come two woes more hereafter.

The first two woes occur during the seals and during the time of the parallel last three trumpets. When John *sees* the vision of the woes, remember, we are in an *interlude*. The angels are getting *ready* to sound the seventh trumpet. John *envisioned* the woes when there was one more seal to open *before* the sky rolls up like a scroll and the stars fall. When John saw a vision, he reported what he saw, but the order of his reporting is *not* to depict sequential events.

Remember, John was told to write what he *sees*, but he also adds what he *hears*. Sometimes they show two different "pictures." One vision may be symbolic, while the other a literal interpretation (e.g., 144,000 is a *symbolic* number, while "a great multitude, which no man could number" is a literal *interpretation*.)

Trumpet 6

13 And the sixth angel sounded, and I heard a voice from the four horns of the golden altar which is before God,
14 Saying to the sixth angel which had the trumpet, Loose the four angels which are bound in the great river Euphrates.

Like the murderous demonic locusts that were loosed from their confinement to torment the wicked, these four fallen angels are also being loosed from confinement for that very purpose as well. These are very terrible and murderous fallen angels. These are probably the fallen angels that God has kept in eternal bonds under darkness for the judgment of the great day. They are mentioned in Jude 6.

15 And the four angels were loosed, which were prepared for an hour, and a day, and a month, and a year, for to slay the third part of men.
16 And the number of the army of the horsemen *were* two hundred thousand: thousand and I heard the number of them.

The army of 200,000,000 is *not* a literal number. It denotes a numberless host. This number signifies an *exceedingly large* company of warriors. Perhaps this army even includes fallen angelic beings. Whether or not that is true, it's not likely *the point* of this passage. However, an army of such magnitude would most likely *not* be 100 percent of human origin. What should we take away from this as the *main* point? For one thing, it should scare every lukewarm pretender into a full surrender to God. God is *not* playing.

17 And thus I saw the horses in the vision, and them that sat on them, having breastplates of fire, and of jacinth, and brimstone: and the heads of the horses *were* as the heads of lions; and out of their mouths issued fire and smoke and brimstone.

The vision of the horsemen and their horses is a dark and terrible scene of what awaits the doomed. While we now live in the days of *grace and mercy*, passages like this should scare the daylights out of anyone moving *away* from God and dabbling in sin. *Today is the day of repentance and grace.* Tomorrow is not promised.

18 By these three was the third part of men killed, by the fire, and by the smoke, and by the brimstone, which issued out of their mouths.

Fire, smoke, and brimstone is tied to the *second death* experience of all unrepentant rebels at the *end* of the "millennium" of our day. *Only* the overcomers, the *redeemed* Church, will *not* experience the second death.

> **Rev. 2:11** He that overcometh shall not be hurt of the second death.

The *fire* of these verses is *figurative*, just as it is in other verses throughout the Bible. One of those other verses with *figurative fire* is in the book of Jeremiah.

Jer. 5:14 Wherefore thus saith the LORD God of hosts, Because ye speak this word, behold, I will make my words in thy mouth fire, and this people wood, and it shall devour them.

The *words* of the "two witnesses" are said to have the ultimate effect of *devouring* people.

19 For their power is in their mouth, and in their tails: for their tails *were* like unto serpents, and had heads, and with them they do hurt. 20 And the rest of the men which were not killed by these plagues yet repented not of the works of their hands, that they should not worship devils, and idols of gold, and silver, and brass, and stone, and of wood: which neither can see, nor hear, nor walk:

Isaiah 41:29 Behold, they are all vanity; their works are nothing: their molten images are wind and confusion.

1 Corinthians 10:20 But *I say,* that the things which the Gentiles sacrifice, they sacrifice to devils, and not to God: and I would not that ye should have fellowship with devils.

The *plagues* we read about in Revelation are *intended* to bring the spiritually blind, religiously deceived, earth-dwellers, agnostics, God-haters, and *all* sinners *to repentance.* In the Old Testament times, sinful people responded to God's redemptive judgments by turning back to God.

Jeremiah 14:21-22 For the sake of Your name do not despise us; do not disgrace Your glorious throne. Remember Your covenant with us; do not break it. Can the worthless idols of the nations bring rain? Do the skies alone send showers? Is this not by You, O LORD our God? So we put our hope in You, for You have done all these things.

They were sorry. They <u>turned</u> from their sin. But John says in Revelation 9:20 that in the *last* days many people *will not* repent. God has always allowed suffering and judgments to cause people and nations to repent and turn from their sins. His judgments start as *redemptive*, with mercy and restoration. As time progresses toward the day of wrath, and people *refuse* to repent, God's judgments will be more *punitive*, frequent, and severe.

Revelation 9:15 and 16, like the rest of John's visions, depict *figurative language*. The point of these passages is *not* for us try to fit our modern-day warfare capabilities and numbers into John's vision. A *two-hundred-million-man army* is massively greater—200 times greater—than our *entire* Department of Defense. But perhaps that number is the number of all the "army men" over *all* time since creation. That large number simply means that John saw *a massive army*. Since the fall of man, this conglomerate, *unregenerated* "army" has killed approximately *one third* of the people on the entire planet. The unredeemed "armies" of all godless rulers have targeted followers of God since the first century. Revelation 9:20 shows the *result* of the judgments in verses 17 and 18. The earth-dwellers *repented not*. They *would not* repent of *any* of their wickedness.

From the hardened sinner to the self-deceived religious hypocrite, many people are *willingly* ignorant of the true character and nature of Jesus Christ. They do not care to know *their only rescue*. The lives and testimonies of many *false* Christians are lives of deception. They rest their hope in some imaginary "scales" tipping in their favor, finding more good in them than bad. They *do* want to be rescued, but they love *the world* and still want popularity, power, and prosperity more than anything. The reality of Jesus Christ's second coming is not a reality to them. (Preparation is the evidence of belief. No preparation— no belief.) The Bible and prophecy just seems too divisive, so they avoid it. They seek worldly pundits who will make them feel a false hope that *this world* can one day be healed through the unity of all mankind. But there is *no* unity between the harlot and the bride, the defiled and the redeemed, the righteous and the unrighteous.

Unity was one of the earliest, great *deceptions* of Satan. The tower of Babel was a tower of unity, leading to heaven. While the unconverted *want* to go to heaven, they also want license to keep their sin and rule their own lives. They want all God's gifts but not God. God must *destroy* the corrupt world system which the earth-dwellers love so much, because it is hopelessly opposed to Him, and it *cannot* be converted.

God sent His Son, Jesus Christ to *save* the world. *The whole Bible is the story of God's redemption of mankind.* God's plan is a story of love, grace, mercy, a call to repentance, redemptive judgments for those who resist His mercy, punishment for stubborn rebels against God, a last call, and finally utter destruction and *eternal* punishment of all who oppose Him. *The redemption plan of God will be complete and eternal on the last day.*

It *is* possible for the conclusion of this age to begin while many of the prophets and preachers, along with the saints, and the earth-dwellers alike, will be *unaware* of this reality, simply because it is not playing out like popular Christian books about the time of tribulation, or Hollywood scripts from "Christian" pretribulation movies.

21 Neither repented they of their murders, nor of their sorceries, nor of their fornication, nor of their thefts.

At this point, seals 1–5 are in progress, with trumpets 1–6. Trumpet 6 has sounded. *The last seal will now be broken,* and the angel in Revelation 5, will hand the *open* scroll to another *mighty* angel in Revelation 10.

This scroll symbolizes the worthy Lamb of God's *right* to possess the earth. On this scroll, the thoughts and deeds *of all mankind, over all time*, are before God. This is a sober legal recording.

CHAPTER 14

The Seven Thunders Mystery and One Giant Angel

<u>Revelation 10</u>

1 And I saw another mighty angel come down from heaven, clothed with a cloud: and a rainbow *was* upon his head, and his face *was* as it were the sun, and his feet as pillars of fire:
2 And he had in his hand a little book open: and he set his right foot upon the sea, and *his* left *foot* on the earth,

D o you see how extraordinary and huge this angel is? This little "book" is the opened scroll. John sees this book as little because it is in the hands of this enormous angel.

3 And cried with a loud voice, as *when* a lion roareth: and when he had cried, seven thunders uttered their voices.
4 And when the seven thunders had uttered their voices, I was about to write: and I heard a voice from heaven saying unto me, seal up those things which the seven thunders uttered, and write them not.

Don't let anyone ever try to tell you what the seven thunders uttered because **they don't know.** God would *not* let John write down what they said.

5 And the angel which I saw stand upon the sea and upon the earth lifted up his hand to heaven,
6 And sware by him that liveth for ever and ever, who created heaven, and the things that therein are, and the earth, and the things that therein are, and the sea, and the things which are therein, that there should be time no longer:

There is no more delay once this trumpet blows. This age will come to a conclusion *at* this seventh trumpet, and *the mystery of God* will be *fulfilled* at that very moment. There is not one minute of time in between.

7 But in the days of the voice of the seventh angel, when he shall begin to sound, the mystery of God should be finished, as he hath declared to his servants the prophets.

> **Ephesians 1:1-3** For this reason I, Paul, the prisoner of Christ Jesus for the sake of you Gentiles Surely you have heard about the administration of God's grace that was given to me for you, that is, the mystery made known to me by revelation, as I have already written briefly.

> **Ephesians 1:7-10** In him we have redemption through his blood, the forgiveness of our trespasses, according to the riches of his grace, which he lavished upon us, in all wisdom and insight. making known to us the mystery of his will, according to his purpose, which he set forth in Christ as a

plan for the fullness of time, to unite all things in him, things in heaven and things on earth.

Revelation 11:15 And the seventh angel sounded; and there were great voices in heaven, saying, The kingdoms of this world are become the kingdoms of our Lord, and of his Christ; and he shall reign for ever and ever.

Revelation 11:15 is the "*mystery of God*" being fulfilled. *The mystery is that it has always been God's plan to unite the kingdoms of earth and the kingdom of heaven, where Christ would reign forever and ever.* Since creation, God has been preparing this eternal kingdom for His son, Jesus Christ, who came to Earth and gave His own blood for this kingdom, in order that He could rule and reign in it forever, where rebellion would *never* rise up again. Entrance into this eternal kingdom is *only* for those who freely accept Jesus Christ as their Lord and Savior, and His blood sacrifice for their rescue.

Nahum 1:9 What do ye imagine against the Lord? he will make an utter end: affliction shall not rise up the second time.

Every time we pray the Lord's Prayer, we are praying that the mystery of God would be finished, and the seventh trumpet would sound. "Thy kingdom come, Thy will be done in earth, as it is in heaven" (Matt. 6:10).

There is a new world coming when the mystery is finished.

Matthew 12:32 And whosoever speaketh a word against the Son of man, it shall be forgiven him: but whosoever speaketh against the Holy Ghost, it shall not be forgiven him, neither in this world, neither in the world to come.

God's plan, from the very beginning of creation, was to redeem a devoted people unto Himself, *out of all the nations.* He chose Israel as the nation through which His blessings would flow to *all* the nations. He also chose one girl, from one nation, to carry the seed of the living God in her womb. That was an honor given to a young Jewish girl named Mary. Mary's husband, Joseph, descended from King David. He was the legal *adoptive* father of Jesus, thereby making Jesus a legal descendant of King David. (Not through a *genetic* connection. Very relevant, as *no one is God's child, spouse, bride, Church, chosen, or body by a genetic connection.)*

Abraham and Sarah gave birth to a son, Isaac. Isaac and Rebekah gave birth to a son, Jacob, who became the father of twelve sons, who represent the twelve tribes of Israel. Jacob and his first wife, Leah, gave birth to a son, Judah, and out of Judah, comes Boaz who was father to Obed, and then from him, Jesse, and from Jesse, David. *David's offspring leads to Joseph, the earthly husband of Mary, the mother of Jesus.*

Again, when Joseph married Mary, he became *the legal father* of Jesus, his adopted son (because his own blood and genetics were not in Jesus.) Out of this union, Jesus is considered to be a *legal* descendent of King David. Jesus is a legal heir of both King David and Abraham. While Jesus didn't descend through his earthly father's blood line, *genetically*, he is still a legal descendant of both King David and Abraham. *And like Jesus, Christian Gentiles are considered by God as legal children of Abraham as well. We are adopted.*

Genesis 22:18 Of Abraham's seed, the word of God says: And in thy seed shall all the nations of the earth be blessed; because thou hast obeyed my voice.

Genesis 12:3b And in thee shall all the families of the earth be blessed.

The Lord spoke to Abraham and said:

Genesis 17:6–9 As for me, behold, my covenant is with thee, and thou shalt be a father of many nations. Neither shall thy name any more be called Abram, but thy name shall be Abraham; for a father of many nations have I made thee. And I will make thee exceeding fruitful, and I will make nations of thee, and kings shall come out of thee. And I will establish my covenant between me and thee and thy seed after thee in their generations for an everlasting covenant, to be a God unto thee, and to thy seed after thee. And I will give unto thee, and to thy seed after thee, the land wherein thou art a stranger, all the land of Canaan, for an everlasting possession; and I will be their God. And God said unto Abraham, Thou shalt keep my covenant therefore, thou, and thy seed after thee in their generations.

God chose the seed of Abraham for his peculiar treasure. "For the LORD hath chosen Jacob unto himself, *and Israel* for his peculiar treasure" (Ps. 135:4). Nevertheless, Scripture also informs us that he chose *Israel* to bless *all* the nations of the earth.

Romans 4:16 Therefore it is of faith that it might be according to grace, so that the promise might be sure to all the seed, not only to those who are of the law, but also to those who are of the faith of Abraham, who is the father of us all.

Romans 9:8 This means that it is not the children of the flesh who are the children of God, but the children of the promise are counted as offspring.

Read that again.

Here is another part of the mystery of God:

Ephesians 3:3-6 How that by revelation he made known unto me the mystery; (as I wrote afore in few words, Whereby, when ye read, ye may understand my knowledge in the mystery of Christ) Which in other ages was not made known unto the sons of men, as it is now revealed unto his holy apostles and prophets by the Spirit; That the Gentiles should be fellow heirs, and of the same body, and partakers of his promise in Christ by the gospel:

And of the same body.

8 And the voice which I heard from heaven spake unto me again, and said, Go *and* take the little book which is open in the hand of the angel which standeth upon the sea and upon the earth.

This is *the opened scroll,* which is the history of the world since creation. Again, this is *not* a literal *book. It is a divine, legal record kept by God of all man's doings.*

9 And I went unto the angel, and said unto him, Give me the little book. And he said unto me, Take *it,* and eat it up; and it shall make thy belly bitter, but it shall be in thy mouth sweet as honey.

10 And I took the little book out of the angel's hand, and ate it up; and it was in my mouth sweet as honey: and as soon as I had eaten it, my belly was bitter.

The Sweet:

Revelation 7:15-17 Therefore they are before the throne of God, and serve Him day and night in His temple. And He who sits on the throne will dwell among them. They shall neither hunger anymore nor thirst anymore; the sun shall not strike them, nor any heat; For the Lamb which is in the midst of the throne shall feed them, and shall lead them unto living fountains of waters: and God shall wipe away all tears from their eyes.

The Bitter:

Revelation 17:5–6a And upon her forehead was a name written, MYSTERY, BABYLON THE GREAT, THE MOTHER OF HARLOTS AND ABOMINATIONS OF THE EARTH. And I saw the woman drunken with the blood of the saints, and with the blood of the martyrs of Jesus:

11 And he said unto me, Thou must prophesy again before many peoples, and nations, and tongues, and kings.

Why must John continue to prophesy? Because there is more to be written. More to be told to the earth-dweller *nations* and *kings* (the world leaders.) The Revelation of Jesus Christ is not complete yet. The rest of the prophecy given to John must specifically address the nations and their *leaders*.

Now comes another interlude.

Pretty much everything John writes about after chapter ten, will focus on the time of the seventh trumpet, at the *end*, or John will have a flashback vision and fill in the gaps of what has already been partially revealed in Revelation 1–10, during the seal and trumpet judgments.

Ch. 11 is where we will learn about the "two" witnesses, and *the seventh trumpet at the end.*

Ch. 12 is where we will see a vision of the ongoing cosmic struggle against "*the woman,*" (or the true "Church" of God, his whole family) and the eventual defeat of the devil, by Jesus Christ *at the end*

Ch. 13 is more information about the first and second beast, which takes place *during* the time of the seal and trumpet judgments.

Ch. 14 is where we learn about three angelic messages and *the harvest of the Earth at the end.*

Ch. 15 informs us about seven angels preparing for the seven last plagues, the bowl judgments. which are *at the end*.

Ch. 16 is the seven bowl judgments of God's wrath on the wicked earth dwellers, *at the end.*

Ch. 17 is an interlude about the identity and predicted doom of Babylon the Great, the beast and false prophet, the kings of the Earth and the nations, and all the godless systems of wicked mankind, who are being punished *during* these seal and trumpet judgments. Their doom is *at the end.*

Ch. 18 is about the fall of Babylon, *at the end.*

Ch. 19 shows the return of Jesus Christ and the marriage supper of the Lamb, *at the end.*

Ch. 20 is about Satan being defeated, and the Great White Throne judgment, *at the end.*

Ch. 21 shows the creation of a new heaven and a new Earth—and a new Jerusalem coming down, *at the end.*

Ch. 22 shows the river of life, and also proclaims some final declarations of blessings and warnings from Jesus Christ—*at the end.*

CHAPTER 15

One Body of Two Witnesses and the Day of the Rapture

Revelation 11

1 And there was given me a reed like unto a rod: and the angel stood, saying, Rise, and measure the temple of God, and the altar, and them that worship therein.

> **Revelation 21:22** And I saw **no temple** therein: for the Lord **God Almighty and the Lamb** are *the temple* of it.

2 But the court which is without the temple leave out, and measure it not; for it is given unto the Gentiles: and the holy city shall they tread under foot forty *and* two months.

This period of forty-two months, also called three and a half years, is *half of the symbolic seven years*, which is a *perfect and complete amount of time*, or the amount of time necessary to conquer evil. This amount of time, forty-two months, *symbolizes* a broken, or uncertain, period of time, but it is a finite time. Seven years represents the *whole* period of the world's existence, since the fall of man, the "thousand years," since creation, during which the Church has always suffered oppression, persecution, and tribulation. The *holy city* is always associated with God's people, "the *New Jerusalem,*" in John's visions.

The *twelve hundred and sixty days* in Revelation 11:3 and 13:5 denotes the same period that is referred to as *forty and two months* in Revelation 11:2. Revelation 12:6 calls this time "*twelve hundred and sixty days,*" and Revelation 12:14 "*a time, and times, and half a time.*" "A time" is *one year*, "times" is *two years*, and a "half time" is a *half year.* That equals three and a half years, or twelve hundred and sixty days. These symbolic expressions of time are also found in Daniel 7:25 and Daniel 12:7.

> **Daniel 7:25** And he shall speak great words against the most High, and shall wear out the saints of the most High, and think to change times and laws: and they shall be given into his hand until a time and times and the dividing of time.

> **Daniel 12:7** And I heard the man clothed in linen, which was upon the waters of the river, when he held up his right hand and his left hand unto heaven, and sware by him that liveth for ever that it shall be for a time, times, and an half; and when he shall have accomplished to scatter the power of the holy people, all these things shall be finished.

The *temple* in Revelation 11:1 is to be interpreted symbolically since it is no longer used for sacrifices, as in the old covenant, and which pointed to the coming Lamb of God. The temple was destroyed in AD 70. The temple is used as *a type* of the holy *people* of God's Church, which John continually represents in his apocalyptic writings. *We* are that temple. (1 Cor. 3:17; 2 Cor. 6:16; Eph.. 2:19–22) Read it.

The *physical temple* was once known as the dwelling place of God, and it was the place in which God was to be worshipped. This verse is *not* pointing to a future rebuilt physical temple. There are *no* measurements. This is all figurative language from the master of figurative language, Jesus. Let me ask you this. If the *unbelieving Jews did* rebuild the temple, would God come and occupy it? No. Don't get hung up on turning *figurative language* into something literal. The contemporary city of Jerusalem is *not* a holy city. *We are that "holy city".*

In verses 1–2, John is directed to measure the symbolic temple, *the worshippers,* and he is told to *leave out* the outer court. The *left-out portion* represents the faithless, apostate portion of the *visible* Church of God, seen in organized, lukewarm, and faithless *religion. In all of John's apocalyptic visions and writings, the temple and Jerusalem are figurative of God's people and are never literal.* The *measuring* is to *juxtaposition* the elect, faithful and *genuine* part of the church from the nominal, worldly, and lukewarm part—the ones who will *not* heed God's warning to the Church to *repent.* The measuring is also a *metaphor* to signify that God will employ a careful investigation and scrutiny of His people. God takes notice of the ones who are measured and sealed. *Those who are measured and sealed will be preserved from the "sore judgments" and "the hour of temptation"* (Rev. 3:10).

When God measures, He uses a plumb line. When God holds the plumb line next to His people, He is serious. He is looking for people who are perfectly upright, who are fitly built, who are *faithful,* and who pass the test. None of us would pass the test, *but for God's grace through Jesus Christ.* We would *all* fall short and be condemned by our own sins and cast away from the presence of God for ever. But Jesus took our sin and our punishment upon Himself. *God's perfect justice is fulfilled in Him alone.* Galatians 2:16b says, *"by the works of the law shall no flesh be justified."* Galatians 2:21b says, *"if righteousness is come by the law, then Christ is dead in vain."* When God measures, will He see Christ in you? That's what it takes to be perfectly upright.

Progressing through the book of Revelation, we are now on the cusp of the last day. *The seventh trumpet is prepared to sound,* and the bowls of God's wrath are ready to be poured on all earth-dwellers. God's warning through John makes it crystal clear that all those who refuse to repent will be utterly destroyed and then cast into the devil's hell forever. God's final judgment, His fury and wrath, comes with no mercy at all. The days of grace and mercy will have expired.

No one has the promise of a tomorrow. If you are not in right relationship with God, *today* is the day of salvation. I'm not talking about simply getting active in a church or rallying behind Christian politicians. I'm talking about seeking a true *relationship* with God. Repent of any sin in your life. Read His Word, and commune with Him. Love what He loves and hate what He hates. Jesus is not only our Savior; He is our *Lord.*

There are *many* churchgoers who have very little appetite to spend personal, quiet time with God in their own homes. Their preferred method of "knowing" God is through the preaching and teachings of *others,* preferably on Sunday morning, one day a week. Rarely do they *study* the Word of God for themselves. Rarely do they truly take the personal, quiet time *to meditate on* God's holy Word and let it impact their lives. God's Word is a *living* Word, and it *should* impact the hearts and lives of *all* yielded vessels. No impact—not yielded.

Individuals make up the Church, not bricks and mortar. The Church is not simply a club for friendships and feel-good messages, or sermons imploring improved morality. It is an assembly of people who congregate to *worship* God. *It is about God.*

It's not enough to know *about* God. We must *know* God and be in a *right relationship* with Him. God is a holy God. We must renounce all sin and live for Him every day. The cost will seem too high for those who love the world, or who love their secret sins. While the truth of God's impending judgment of all sinners torments the guilty internally, many will still *refuse* to rise above their sin and lukewarmness.

How and why does God want the *worshippers* to be *measured* in Revelation 11:1? God is measuring for *enduring, genuine faith* in His only begotten son, Jesus Christ. There is *no* faith in the faithless, self-deceived *cowards, who cling to the world* and hate the rejection of the earth-dwellers who *seem* to be the successful and favored in society. The *faithless* portion of the visible Church or temple, is symbolically called *Gentiles* in Revelation 11:2, as a figurative representation of all that is worldly. God spoke to the complete Church through the seven Asian churches in the beginning of Revelation. There will be those who do not heed God's last words and warnings to the Church. Unrepentant members of the *visible* Church are typified by the *outer court* and numbered among the *unholy* who are left out.

Remember the story of Cain and Abel's sacrifice? What was the lesson of this story? Worship that comes from *self-efforts* (works) and not of faith is not acceptable to God. *God does not dwell in faithless temples.* The outer courtyard of the temple is a depiction of the worldly, who do *not* have a true relationship with God. Many in our visible Churches today are in the outer courtyard. They may appear to be "good" as far as their *visible* works and service, but these same ones seek to establish *their own* righteousness. Some in the visible Church might whole-heartedly believe *in* God, but don't really *believe* God. That doesn't work. Others in the *visible* Church acknowledge God in *words but deny him in obedience.* That doesn't work either.

Sadly, hordes of people in one of the largest sects of organized *religion* in America and in the world are in the unmeasured courtyard of the temple. They are among the *faithless* Gentiles because they have no faith in the *completed* work of Jesus Christ on the Cross of Calvary. Just as Eve was beguiled by the subtlety of Satan in the Garden of Eden, it is certain that the devil has lost none of his persuasive arts that operate through *deception.* Satan *always* aims to rob God of his disciples *by supplanting the gospel of grace with the law.* Only the *genuine* family of God accepts God's grace, *apart from the law.* All of the apostate religions in the world operate under the law. God's grace is not enough for the apostate Church, so *they add works*, removing themselves from God's grace.

Some religions seek to appease God through other means than the Cross of Christ. Their members seek to please God by wearing medals and scapulars. They collect holy cards as objects of veneration and pray repetitious prayers with beads. They seek audience with God through other mediators besides

Jesus Christ. They seek to acquire favor and *earn* mercy and grace through *service* and *sacrifice* because they view these religious duties as satisfactory and compensatory to God. They do not comprehend righteousness by faith in Christ.

Most are kind-hearted, reverent, churchgoing people to us, but in truth, they are *rejectors* of Jesus Christ's exclusive, exhaustive, effectual, blood sacrifice as the *full* atonement for their sins. They have added *other ways* to appropriate God's grace. There is only *one* way to God, through Jesus Christ. He is the *only* mediator between man and God, and the *only* means of atonement for sin. He has *no helpers*, and no co-redeemer. *All* who seek *another way* to acquire God's grace and mercy are called *thieves and robbers.*

John 10:1 Verily, verily, I say unto you, He that entereth not by the door into the sheepfold, but climbeth up some other way, the same is a thief and a robber.

John 10:7 Then said Jesus unto them again, Verily, verily, I say unto you, I am the door of the sheep.

Romans 10:3 For they being ignorant of God's righteousness, and going about to establish their own righteousness, have not submitted themselves unto the righteousness of God.

Isaiah 64:6 But we are all as an unclean *thing,* and all our righteousnesses *are* as filthy rags; and we all do fade as a leaf; and our iniquities, like the wind, have taken us away.

Matthew 10:32-33 Whosoever therefore shall confess me before men, him will I confess also before my Father which is in heaven. But whosoever shall deny me before men, him will I also deny before my Father which is in heaven.

Titus 1:16 They profess that they know God; but in works they deny *him*, being abominable, and disobedient, and unto every good work reprobate.

In Revelation 18:2, John wasn't to merely "*leave out*," the outer court in his measurements, but to "*cast out*." This disqualified area signifies a part that is *within* the true Church but *isn't* the true Church. These "Gentiles" who possess the outer court of the temple are *spiritually separated* from the true believers *yet aren't even aware*. They have sold out to or bought into the philosophies of *their religious institutions,* which are at enmity with God. *They love their deception and are not faithful servants of the true God and His gospel.* They have created their own God and gospel, which they like much more.

The apostate Church is *self-*deceived and blind. They attempt to establish *their own* righteousness by *their own* works. They will *not* believe in the miracle of Jesus' *finished* work on the cross. They have no assurance of salvation, and therefore seek to achieve the favor of God through *their* service, prayers, sacrifices, and in *their* membership and participation in *their* religion.

Sadly, these apostate "Gentiles" will be left behind when the redeemed, true, elect, blood-bought, Church of Jesus Christ is caught up to be with the Lord in the air.

3 And I will give *power* unto my two witnesses, and they shall prophesy a thousand two hundred *and* threescore days, clothed in sackcloth.

There is always diversity of interpretation in regard to the *figurative* numbers John used in Revelation. Chapter 11, I believe, is *inspired allegory* intended to convey *spiritual* teachings applicable to every age. The symbolic events and persons in chapter 11 depict likenesses of actual events and persons recorded in the Old Testament Scriptures.

The *two witnesses* are *all* the *representatives of the elect Church of God*, embracing both (1) *Jewish* and (2) *Christian* believers. You might want to read that again.

Here is why it *is not probable, nor conceivable that the "two" witnesses are simply two men,* namely, Moses and Elijah. *Revelation is not a literal book.* John's entire vision is to be understood as symbolical, especially all of the *numbers.* There is no pattern, nor scriptural reference of God ever *returning* anyone from heaven to earth to suffer as these "two witnesses" will suffer. Revelation 11:8 says, "And their dead bodies shall lie in the street of the great city, which spiritually is called Sodom and Egypt, where also our Lord was crucified." *Sodom and Egypt* are *metaphorical* of wicked places. This city and country are not the actual place of Christ's crucifixion. They are symbolical types of what is *evil.*

These *"two witnesses"* being *literally two men* reaching the whole earth is hardly likely. No more likely than the Lord's literal crucifixion being in Sodom or Egypt. John's vision of the two witnesses expresses *a type*, patterned from the public, bold, and faithful witness of both *Moses and Elijah*. Both men suffered much hardship, were preserved by the mighty hand of God, and ultimately were vindicated. *God's witnesses in the last days of time will also suffer, be preserved, and will be vindicated in the end.*

All of God's faithful people are given *power* by God to witness and prophecy. The symbolic apparel of God's holy people is represented by mourning sackcloth because it is distressful and mournful to witness to haughty rebels who sneer, mock, and also persecute the messengers, but will **not** repent. God is not willing that *any* should perish. We would *not* be assigned to witness *if there was no one left for God to rescue,* so we *know* that there *will be* some who *will* believe our testimony and be saved.

> **1 Thessalonians 1:10** When he shall come to be glorified in his saints, and to be admired in all them that believe (because our testimony among you was believed) in that day.

4 These are the two olive trees, and the two candlesticks standing before the God of the earth.

The *two olive trees* represent the Holy Spirit, which is the *fuel* for *the candlesticks* (the light), representing the Church. The source of all light and power for the Church is found in God and in His Word. We also see "the candlestick" with seven lamps in Zechariah's vision in Zechariah 4. His vision shows that the lamps needed no human effort to keep them supplied. They were fed by a fountain above, with seven pipes (the perfect and complete amount) pouring the right amount of *oil* into each of them continually. Without any of man's works or efforts, *God* supplies man with all that he needs to be victorious and eternal children of God. The oil is also figurative of God's grace. Please take the time to read Zechariah 4:1–7 and 4:11–14.

"The candelabrum is a symbol of the Jewish Church and theocracy, in accordance with the imagery in the Apocalypse, where the seven candlesticks are seven Churches (Revelation 1:20). It is made of gold as precious in God's sight, and to be kept pure and unalloyed; it is placed in the sanctuary, and has seven lamps, to indicate that it is bright with the grace of God, and is meant to shed its light around at all times, as Christian men are bidden to shine like lights in the world (Matthew 5:16; Philippians 2:15). The oil that supplies the lamps is the grace of God, the influence of the Holy Spirit, which alone enables the Church to shine and to accomplish its appointed work. The two olive trees are the two authorities, viz. the civil and sacerdotal, through which God communicates his grace to the Church; these stand by the Lord Because, instituted by him, they carry out his will in the ordering, guiding, extending, and purifying his kingdom among men. The two olive branches remit their oil into one receptacle, because the two authorities, the regal and priestly, are intimately connected and united, and their action tends to one end, the promotion of God's glory in the salvation of men. In Messiah these offices are united; he is the channel of Divine grace, the source of light to the whole world." [4]

Pulpit Commentary, Zechariah 4:14

In Revelation 1:20, the two candlesticks stand for the entire redeemed Church: (1) Christians, and (2) redeemed Jews. These together are God's two witnesses on earth. John informed us who the candlesticks were all the way at the beginning of Revelation (1:20).

5 And if any man will hurt them, fire proceedeth out of their mouth, and devoureth their enemies: and if any man will hurt them, he must in this manner be killed.

This *fire* is likely not literal but is *symbolic of the torment of condemnation* felt by those who reject the testimony of the "two witnesses." God will slay his enemies through the prophesying "two witnesses" who will severely denounce the haughty earth-dwellers and their open sin as they *boldly* profess the *truth* of the inerrant, perfect, and immutable Word of God.

> **Jeremiah 5:14** Wherefore thus saith the LORD God of hosts, Because ye speak this word, behold, I will make my words in thy mouth fire, and this people wood, and it shall devour them.

> **Jeremiah 1:9** Then the LORD put forth his hand, and touched my mouth. And the LORD said unto me, Behold, I have put my words in thy mouth. See, I have this day set thee over the nations and over the kingdoms, to root out, and to pull down, and to destroy, and to throw down, to build, and to plant.

6 These have power to shut heaven, that it rain not in the days of their prophecy: and have power over waters to turn them to blood, and to smite the earth with all plagues, as often as they will.

Both Moses and Elijah had power to bring affliction to the earth. This verse intends for God's holy people to understand that the same power that supported God's appointed witnesses in the days of old will also support his people in the days of tribulation. The witnesses (all genuine believers) will have the power to boldly denounce evil-doers, and announce impending and *certain* destruction to all those who reject and despise their prophecy.

1 Kings 17:1 And *Elijah* the Tishbite, *who was* of the inhabitants of Gilead, said unto Ahab, *As* the LORD God of Israel liveth, before whom I stand, there shall not be dew nor rain these years, but according to my word.

Exodus 7:20 And *Moses* and Aaron did so, as the LORD commanded; and he lifted up the rod, and smote the waters that *were* in the river, in the sight of Pharaoh, and in the sight of his servants; and all the waters that *were* in the river were turned to blood.

7 And when they shall have finished their testimony, the beast that ascendeth out of the bottomless pit shall make war against them, and shall overcome them, and kill them.

Satan will come against *all* genuine believers, even killing many. But some will remain alive on earth to accomplish God's work.

The Church's testimony for God will only be finished when there is no more opportunity for repentance. At this point, the hardened criminals and rebellious earth-dwellers, working under the guidance of the antichrist beast, will seemingly make an end of God's holy people by killing them.

8 And their dead bodies *shall lie* in the street of the great city, which spiritually is called Sodom and Egypt, where also our Lord was crucified.

This great city is *not* referring to the New Jerusalem, but to the evil spirit of Babylon. To leave the bodies lying in the street, with no burials, is a brazen display of contempt and hatred. The unrepentant masses and the Antichrist will be so proud of their accomplishment. The Church is finally slaughtered. (Or so they think.)

9 And they of the people and kindreds and tongues and nations shall see their dead bodies three days and an half, and shall not suffer their dead bodies to be put in graves.

The earth-dwellers will be ecstatic that the witnesses' tormenting message of condemnation has finally been silenced, along with all the miraculous signs that confirmed their message. Earth-dwellers despise the lifestyle and message of Christians. They hate our testimony and devotion to God. They especially hate prophecy of God's impending judgment on *them*, unless they repent. They *hate* God and hate His Church. Many would not admit this, but they do.

10 And they that dwell upon the earth shall rejoice over them, and make merry, and shall send gifts one to another; because these two prophets tormented them that dwelt on the earth.
11 And after three days and an half the Spirit of life from God entered into them, and they stood upon their feet; and great fear fell upon them which saw them.

The earth-dwellers will hold celebrations all across the world for their perceived victory because they think the torment will now stop. But this is the *last* celebration they will ever have. It only lasts for *a brief time*. Three and a half days is a symbolic number for a *brief* period of time.

So, we have made it all the way through Revelation 11 to discover that it is not just *two* men, Moses and Elijah, who will be *the sole witnesses* to the worldwide masses of unrepentant sinners. *Two men would not make much impact on the billions worldwide.* And don't believe they would be allowed to witness through the *media.* The media is *already* cutting off the voice of God's people, and it is getting worse daily. There are billions of people in the world, and there are faithful believers who dwell among the masses in *every* nation. *This remnant company of all elect believers are the witnesses.*

Can you even imagine the *actual* scenario of *God's entire remnant Church* lying dead in streets all across the world? Imagine a brief time later, when every single one of the murdered and despised saints stand up, alive again, while *all* graves everywhere are also opening up. The *redeemed* of God are receiving *glorified bodies and going up* to meet Jesus in the air. That's what i**s** going to happen. *That day* is *the d*ay of the Lord—the day that Christ is glorified in the saints. What a glorious day.

Every *earth-dweller* who ever lived and died is *also* now alive again. Their graves also open up. But they do not *rise* to meet the Lord in the air. Every God-rejecting, unrighteous man that ever lived will witness this day. God will *avenge* His bride, His Church, His wife, the New Jerusalem, *and it will be spectacular.*

12 And they heard a great voice from heaven saying unto them, Come up hither. And they ascended up to heaven in a cloud; and their enemies beheld them.

When the seventh trumpet sounds, the graves of the redeemed of every age open up. God's great voice and all His angels and armies *call up* God's eternal family, the faithful Church, both those who *sleep* in Christ and those who are alive and remain. "*Come up hither.*" There will be *great voices* in heaven celebrating with God, shouting, "*The kingdoms of this world are become the kingdoms of our Lord, and of his Christ; and He shall reign for ever and ever.*" This is a glorious and spectacular sight. Imagine this day!

Not only will the *contemporary enemies* of *the martyrs for Christ* witness the Church ascending up to heaven, but *all* enemies of God and his Church, *of every age*, will rise from their graves *to witness this rapture.*

> **Revelation 1:7** Behold, he cometh with clouds; and every eye shall see him, and they also which pierced him: and all kindreds of the earth shall wail because of him. Even so, Amen.

13 And the same hour was there a great earthquake, and the tenth part of the city fell, and in the earthquake were slain of men seven thousand: and the remnant were affrighted, and gave glory to the God of heaven.

This remnant will meet the Lord in the air when He calls.

14 The second woe is past; *and*, behold, the third woe cometh quickly.

The three woes are the last three trumpets. The second and third woe are timed with the seventh trumpet. It all happens *very quickly.* On that day, there will be utter terror, chaos, loud voices and trumpets from heaven, armies in the sky, earthquakes, death, and eternal hopelessness for the lost, following the rescue/rapture of God's people.

Trumpet 7

15 And the seventh angel sounded; and there were great voices in heaven, saying, The kingdoms of this world are become *the kingdoms* of our Lord, and of his Christ; and he shall reign for ever and ever.

Okay. We are halfway through Revelation, yet this is where we read about *the end* again. *This is another vision of the same time of the rapture.*

John will now *circle back* and start a new *interlude.*

16 And the four and twenty elders, which sat before God on their seats, fell upon their faces, and worshipped God,
17 Saying, We give thee thanks, O Lord God Almighty, which art, and wast, and art to come; because thou hast taken to thee thy great power, and hast reigned.
18 And the nations were angry, and thy wrath is come, and the time of the dead, that they should be judged, and that thou shouldest give reward unto thy servants the prophets, and to the saints, and them that fear thy name, small and great; and shouldest destroy them which destroy the earth.
19 And the temple of God was opened in heaven, and there was seen in his temple the ark of his testament: and there were lightnings, and voices, and thunderings, and an earthquake, and great hail.

> **Daniel 12:1** And at that time shall Michael stand up, the great prince which standeth for the children of thy people: and there shall be a time of trouble, such as never was since there was a nation even to that same time: and at that time thy people shall be delivered, every one that shall be found written in the book.

Daniel 12:2 And many of them that sleep in the dust of the earth shall awake, some to everlasting life, and some to shame and everlasting contempt.

Daniel places the deliverance of God's people *during the tribulation,* but *just prior* to God's wrath—the worst time of trouble since there was a nation. The deliverance of God's people, the rapture, *happens in concert with the resurrection of the dead,* which scripture makes *clear* in Revelation 11:18. It all takes place *at Christ's coming.*

CHAPTER 16

The Dragon and the Overcomers

Revelation 12

1 And there appeared a great wonder in heaven; a woman clothed with the sun, and the moon under her feet, and upon her head a crown of twelve stars:

This is *imagery of Eve* and *all of the faithful saints* (God's people) *throughout history*, the whole company of those who believe God—the blood-bought, redeemed Church (Gen. 3:15).

In Revelation 12:6, we see *this woman* is representative of the Church in the last days, during the tribulation period.

The *sun* represents Jesus Christ: *"the light of the world"* (John 8:12).

The moon represents the ancient serpent, Satan, the deceiver of the whole world. The seed of the woman (Jesus) will trample down and destroy the works of the devil (Gen. 1:15).

The redeemed Church will bruise the head of the Devil and will overcome the serpent. The *moon under her feet* shows the Church's victory over Satan's in his attempts to subvert and destroy the Church.

God speaking to the serpent: "I will put enmity between thee and the woman, and between thy seed and her seed; it shall bruise thy head, and thou shalt bruise his heel" (Gen. 3:15).

Those who oppose God and follow Satan are Satan's seed. Those who follow God and do His will are God's seed. The term *"it"* refers to the Church—which is the "seed" of the woman.

> **Romans 16:19-20**—(*Paul speaking to the brethren/the Church*) "I would have you wise unto that which is good, and simple concerning evil. And the God of peace shall bruise Satan under your feet shortly"

The image of the *twelve stars* suggests a reference to *the complete body of Christ*—the *twelve tribes of Israel* through whom God worked to bring the Messiah to earth, and the *twelve apostles*, who later formed the foundation of the *one* true Church.

> **Malachi 4:1-3** For, behold, the day cometh, that shall burn as an oven; and all the proud, yea, and all that do wickedly, shall be stubble: and the day that cometh shall burn them up, saith the LORD of hosts, that it shall leave them neither root nor branch. But unto you that fear my name shall the Sun of righteousness arise with healing in his wings; and **ye** shall go forth, and grow up as calves of the stall. And ye shall tread down the wicked; for they shall be ashes under

the soles of your feet in the day that I shall do this, saith the LORD of hosts.

2 And she being with child cried, travailing in birth, and pained to be delivered.

Eve's seed is Israel, and out of Israel, Eve's seed is *Jesus Christ.* Her descendants lead *to the birth of the Church,* the true followers of the Lamb of God.

3 And there appeared another wonder in heaven; and behold a great red dragon, having seven heads and ten horns, and seven crowns upon his heads.

This *great red dragon* is none other than *the ancient serpent.* This figurative and apocalyptic language is *not* meant to be taken literally.

The symbolism of this *"wonder in heaven"* seems intended to portray all of the ungodly world powers which have oppressed God's people, the Church, and the nation of Jews *throughout all history.* Revelation 17:10, 12 declare that the *heads* and horns typify *kings and kingdoms.* And again, the numbers seven (and often ten) are symbolic of completeness and emanating from God.

In this image of the great red dragon, we have a picture of the complete (seven heads) opposition of the unregenerate world powers, against God and His Church. This power is derived from the devil. The seven crowns are symbols of the dragon's universal sovereignty and worldwide dominion, as "prince of this world," (John 12:31) and the ten horns, symbolic of his despotic power in *all* ages.

4 And his tail drew the third part of the stars of heaven, and did cast them to the earth: and the dragon stood before the woman which was ready to be delivered, for to devour her child as soon as it was born.

These "*stars of heaven*" are approximately one third of the angels in heaven who aligned with Lucifer in rebellion against God (Ezek. 28; Isa. 14:12). The child they sought to devour was Jesus Christ.

The *third part* signifies a considerable number but not the larger part.

5 And she brought forth a man child, who was to rule all nations with a rod of iron: and her child was caught up unto God, and *to* his throne.
6 And the woman fled into the wilderness, where she hath a place prepared of God, that they should feed her there a thousand two hundred *and* threescore days.

The woman, or *the Church* is *in flight* for a symbolic period of *three and a half years,* or forty-two months. This period coincides with Revelation 11:2, depicting the devil's persecution of God's people *in every age.* (Christians are foreign ambassadors in this world.) The three and a half years, or forty-two months, refers to the reign of the Antichrist, specifically, *during the last half of the complete measure of time (symbolic seven years), or since the beginning of the "Church" on the earth.*

7 And there was war in heaven: Michael and his angels fought against the dragon; and the dragon fought and his angels,

8 And prevailed not; neither was their place found any more in heaven.

9 And the great dragon was cast out, that old serpent, called the Devil, and Satan, which deceiveth the whole world: he was cast out into the earth, and his angels were cast out with him.

10 And I heard a loud voice saying in heaven, Now is come salvation, and strength, and the kingdom of our God, and the power of his Christ: for the accuser of our brethren is cast down, which accused them before our God day and night.

11 And they overcame him by the blood of the Lamb, and by the word of their testimony; and they loved not their lives unto the death.

Revelation 12:11 is how the Church will *ultimately* conquer the evil one.

The faithful family of God needs to memorize and practice Revelation 12:11 right now. We must not value our life in this world at the expense of letting our first love cool off or get dim. We must love God *supremely*, even to the extent of accepting death, if necessary, for the sake of obeying Jesus Christ and giving our testimony of Jesus Christ. We must not ever deny Him.

12 Therefore rejoice, *ye* heavens, and ye that dwell in them. Woe to the inhabiters of the earth and of the sea. for the devil is come down unto you, having great wrath, because he knoweth that he hath but a short time.

We have our citizenship in heaven *right now*. We are *heaven-dwellers*, as opposed to earth-dwellers.

13 And when the dragon saw that he was cast unto the earth, he persecuted the woman which brought forth the man *child*.

The devil was defeated in heaven, and cast out (Isa. 14:12). On earth, he directs his attack against *the man child—Jesus* (Rev. 12:5), and against his body—(the woman.) The body of Christ is the Church (Rev. 12:6).

14 And to the woman were given two wings of a great eagle, that she might fly into the wilderness, into her place, where she is nourished for a time, and times, and half a time, from the face of the serpent.

"*Were given*" is the passive voice, which depicts *an action of God*, nourishing His body in the world.

In the Old Testament, *Israel* escaped from Pharaoh and was preserved by God in *the wilderness*. Throughout scripture, even while God's faithful followers are under God's protective provisions, they often continue to bear reproach and tribulations. Until God's perfect plan is fulfilled, in the fulness of time, *we* will continue to bear reproach as well.

> **Exodus 19:4** Ye have seen what I did unto the Egyptians, and how I bare you on eagles' wings, and brought you unto myself

> **Deuteronomy 32:11** As an eagle stirreth up her nest, fluttereth over her young, spreadeth abroad her wings, taketh them, beareth them on her wings 12 *So* the LORD alone did lead him, and *there was* no strange god with him.

Christians have been allowed to grow and thrive over the centuries. *America has been especially blessed of God.* Despite these blessings, America has emerged as the only nation that fits *all* of the descriptions concerning end-time *Babylon* in Jeremiah 50 and 51.

America has also been *Israel's* most powerful and supportive ally since Israel's rebirth in 1948. It could be a coincidence, but maybe not, that *America's national symbol* is that of an *eagle*. Until the last few years, the "eagle" has been a friend and an unwavering ally of Israel, and a *refuge* for Christians to thrive at home. *But now,* the political scene of the world, *which includes America*, is *posturing with deception* for biblical, cataclysmic events surrounding the *national and spiritual Jews*. Don't believe all that you hear on the news. God's history book, the Bible, tells the future much more accurately than the fake news.

15 And the serpent cast out of his mouth water as a flood after the woman, that he might cause her to be carried away of the flood.

> "The flood is typical of every form of destruction with which the devil seeks to overwhelm the Church of God. At the period of the writing of the Apocalypse, it plainly symbolized the bitter persecutions to which Christians were subjected; but its meaning need not be limited to this one form of destruction."[5]

16 And the earth helped the woman, and the earth opened her mouth, and swallowed up the flood which the dragon cast out of his mouth.

This is a picture of the Church being helped and preserved, in a supernatural way, from the overwhelming efforts of the devil. Remember the Old Testament story where God opened up the earth and swallowed up the enemies of His people?

Numbers 16:30 But if the LORD creates something new, and the ground opens its mouth and swallows them up with all that belongs to them, and they go down alive into Sheol, then you shall know that these men have despised the LORD.

Numbers 16:32 And the earth opened its mouth and swallowed them up, with their households and all the people who belonged to Korah and all their goods.

17 And the dragon was wroth with the woman, and went to make war with the remnant of her seed, which keep the commandments of God, and have the testimony of Jesus Christ.

Satan is fuming because he has failed to prevent the mission of Jesus Christ, the man child, so he attempts to persecute and overwhelm the body of Christ. Satan proceeds to use every evil means to attack and bring down the most devout members of God's family—the remnant.

CHAPTER 17

Two Beasts

1 And I stood upon the sand of the sea, and saw a beast rise up out of the sea, having seven heads and ten horns, and upon his horns ten crowns, and upon his heads the name of blasphemy.

This image of the beast is figurative and not meant to describe his bodily form, but rather is meant to convey certain ideas about this powerful entity. This is a man, empowered by Satan. The *nations* of the world, (the sea) under the secular governments and false religions, (heads, horns and crowns) have persecuted the true Church of God *since it was first formed.*

> **Daniel 7:24-25** As for the *ten horns*, out of this kingdom *ten kings* shall arise, *and another shall arise after them;* he shall be different from the former ones, and shall put down three kings. He shall speak words against the Most High, and *shall wear out the saints of the Most High*, and shall think to change the times and the law; and they shall be given into his hand *for a time, times, and half a time.*

The seven heads are symbolic of universal and complete dominion.

At the time of John's writing of the Apocalypse, heathen Rome was the world's chief superpower. They exercised sovereign dominion over the political and religious affairs in society. John's prophecy addresses beyond this one superpower to include all of the God-hating superpowers of all time.

2 And the beast which I saw was like unto a leopard, and his feet were as *the feet* of a bear, and his mouth as the mouth of a lion: and the dragon gave him his power, and his seat, and great authority.

Leopards are very swift and bloodthirsty. *Lions* rule with lordly dominion. *Bears* are forceful and tenacious in their purpose. These were characteristics of the Roman empire at the time of John's vision. While the Roman empire exhibited these very characteristics, this was *not* the identity of the beast described. How do we know this? Because in Revelation 17:8, scripture states that this beast *is not* currently in power (in John's day).

> **Revelation 17:8** The beast that you saw *was, and is not*, and *is about to rise* from the bottomless pit and go to destruction. And *the dwellers on earth* whose names have *not* been written in the book of life from the foundation of the world will marvel to see the beast, because it *was and is not* and *is to come.*

The same oppositional and cruel qualities of leopards, lions, and bears have been exhibited against the Church in every age in history by the persecutors of the God's people. The vision represents the totality of every world empire opposed to Christ and His kingdom.

The *sea* in verse 13:1 represents the *Gentile* nations of earth-dwellers, from which the Beast, or the false messiah comes.

3 And I saw one of his heads as it were wounded to death; and his deadly wound was healed: and all the world wondered after the beast.

"His heads" are factions of his empire. "The wound" is his temporary demise, of some sort. "The world" represents the unregenerate earth-dwellers.

4 And they worshipped the dragon which gave power unto the beast: and they worshipped the beast, saying, Who *is* like unto the beast? who is able to make war with him?

This *worship* is total veneration and respect for *his* visible power, lifting it above the revealed power and attributes of the *true* God of the Universe. The fear of the beast will rule over the fear of God to the earth-dwellers.

5 And there was given unto him a mouth speaking great things and blasphemies; and power was given unto him to continue forty *and* two months.

The devil only holds this power by the will of God. It was *given to him* for "*a little season,*" or *for three and a half years*, which *signifies the period of the world's existence during which the Church is to suffer oppression.* This three and a half years/forty two months, is about *half* of the "seven years," or a long period of time, (in the millennium of Rev. 20) designated by God (Rev. 6:10–11).

6 And he opened his mouth in blasphemy against God, to blaspheme his name, and his tabernacle, and them that dwell in heaven.

He blasphemed against God and *against all those whose citizenship and resting place is in heaven*. Hordes of heaven's citizens will still be residing on earth *among* the earth-dwellers, *but spiritually, we "dwell in heaven"*.

7 And it was given unto him to make war with the saints, and to overcome them: and power was given him over all kindreds, and tongues, and nations.

Many scriptural references make it clear that the "saints" are both the redeemed Gentiles *and* Jews. They are the universal, *one* true body of Jesus Christ, also called the Church.

> **Ephesians 2:8–22 ESV**
> **8** For by grace you have been saved through faith. And this is not your own doing; it is the gift of God,
> **9** not a result of works, so that no one may boast.
> **10** For we are his workmanship, created in Christ Jesus for good works, which God prepared beforehand, that we should walk in them.
> **11** Therefore remember that **at one time** you **Gentiles** in the flesh, called "the uncircumcision" by what is called the circumcision, which is made in the flesh by hands—
> **12** remember that **you were at that time separated from Christ, alienated from the commonwealth of Israel** and **strangers to the covenants of promise,** having no hope and without God in the world.
> **13 But now in Christ Jesus** you **who once were** far off have been brought near by the blood of Christ.

14 For he himself is our peace, who **has made us both one** and has broken down in his flesh the dividing wall of hostility **15** by abolishing the law of commandments expressed in ordinances, **that he might create in himself ONE new man in place of the two**, so making peace, **16** and might **reconcile us both to God in one body** through the cross, thereby killing the hostility. **17** And he came and preached peace to you who were far off and peace to those who were near. **18 For through him we both have access in one Spirit to the Father. 19** So then you are no longer strangers and aliens, but **you are fellow citizens with the saints and members of the household of God, 20** built on **the foundation of the apostles and prophets,** Christ Jesus himself being the cornerstone, **21** in whom **the whole structure, being joined together, grows into a holy temple in the Lord. 22** In him you also are **being built together into a dwelling place for God** by the Spirit.

8 And all that dwell upon the earth shall worship him, whose names are not written in the book of life of the Lamb slain from the foundation of the world.

"The nations" are the instrument by which the complete, universal, faithful, redeemed Church of God is trodden underfoot. There is no immunity from persecution for the Church, and there has never been blanket immunity for God's people in *any* age. This verse is referring to earth-dwellers, not the Church.

9 If any man have an ear, let him hear.

10 He that leadeth into captivity shall go into captivity: he that killeth with the sword must be killed with the sword. Here is the patience and the faith of the saints.

During this period of the world, there are *appointed* sufferings of the elect saints. This is foreordained of God. The saints *will* be overcome, but will ultimately overcome the beast by patience for their deliverance, faith in unseen promises, and the wisdom to not take up carnal arms as their primary defense in opposition of the beast (Rev. 13:10, 18). God will be our avenger! We are not to take up arms to *prevent our suffering at the hands of the beast.* We don't love our lives in this world enough to kill for our "rights." But what about *self*-defense? We always need God's discernment when we must protect the weak and needy. We have a right to defend ourselves, our families, and our homes. We need God's wisdom in *each* situation. Our **conquering** *weapons* will not be the same fatal, earthly weapons used by our foe. **Our** weapons are spiritual and mighty. If our suffering is *God-ordained,* we will *not* be able to prevent it by force of arms. We must stay very close to our Commander-in-Chief, Jesus Christ. He will guide our footsteps.

The Church is to be comforted by *knowing* that God has already pronounced *retaliatory justice* on the wicked who inflict captivity and injustices against His people.

11 And I beheld another beast coming up out of the earth; and he had two horns like a lamb, and he spake as a dragon.

This *second beast* simulates an appearance and authority of a God-sent savior or Messiah, but his words will alert *God's people* of his devilish nature. This beast puts on a pious exterior in order to *deceive.* He performs signs and wonders, and this will *wow* the unsuspecting earth-dwellers to venerate him as divine, the very man whose *symbolic* number is revealed as 666. Since this is not a *literal* number, I won't dwell on *decoding* this number *literally.* John intends for the reader to understand that this number will be associated with some *symbol, or mark of allegiance, to the man of sin.*

This *mark* will identify the one who receives it as someone who is *cooperative* with the powers that be, and is therefore deemed by them as "worthy" to have *access* to goods and services. The *reverse* is true for those who *refuse* the mark. Refusal is essentially a promissory note that one will suffer and probably die when their personal stockpiles run out. Nevertheless, believers are *clearly warned* to *reject the mark,* or whatever the mandated *symbol of allegiance is, at all costs,* even if it means starving to death, imprisonment, or execution.

12 And he exerciseth all the power of the first beast before him, and causeth the earth and them which dwell therein to worship the first beast, whose deadly wound was healed.

The second beast convinces and compels to compliance, *only* the earth-dwellers, or those whose names are *not* written in the book of life of the Lamb. This second beast persuades *unsaved* mankind to worship and pay homage to the first beast. In Revelation 16:13 this second beast is the *false prophet.*

13 And he doeth great wonders, so that he maketh fire come down from heaven on the earth in the sight of men,
14 And deceiveth them that dwell on the earth by *the means of* those miracles which he had power to do in the sight of the beast; saying to

them that dwell on the earth, that they should make an image to the beast, which had the wound by a sword, and did live.

Miracles are never to be our test as to whether something is coming from God. The devil can do miracles. He is allowed this power by God.

15 And he had power to give life unto the image of the beast, that the image of the beast should both speak, and cause that as many as would not worship the image of the beast should be killed.
16 And he causeth all, both small and great, rich and poor, free and bond, to receive a mark in their right hand, or in their foreheads:

Although this second beast, or false prophet, is the *cause* of many people taking the mark of the beast, a number of Bible passages relating to this time of the Apocalypse, show that men have absolute freedom of choice in whom to place their *allegiance*. The beast's worship is *strongly enforced, but not forced.* That is very important. It will be *your* decision. Nevertheless, when *people choose to be deceived* and believe a lie rather than the truth, God *will* turn them over to their own wicked desire for a *delusion,* and they will end up in the devil's eternal hell *for rejecting the truth* that they might be saved. All who will choose to give allegiance to *God* and *not to man* will ultimately face the loss of life. Taking the beast's mark is something one *cannot turn back from.* It is Satan's seal on the receiver's soul.

This second beast symbolizes *self*-deceit. He makes *a strong case* for people to choose the devil's poison. Satan has *most* people in his net *right now.* The people of the nations are caught up in their pleasure-seeking, jet-set lifestyles. They certainly don't want to miss a meal. *Most* will ultimately forfeit their eternal life for the promise of a full belly, just like Esau forsook his birthright for a bowl of porridge. Think about that and weep.

> **2 Thessalonians 2:9–10** The coming of the lawless one is according to the working of Satan, with all power, signs, and lying wonders, And with all deceivableness of unrighteousness in them that perish; because they received not the love of the truth, that they might be saved.

> **2 Thessalonians 2:11–12** And for this cause God shall send them strong delusion, that they should believe a lie: That they all might be damned who believed not the truth, but had pleasure in unrighteousness.

During the tribulation, throughout the entire world, there will be *enforced worship* of a deceptive man of sin, who is empowered by the devil. This man of sin will be a one-world dictator with savage and strong political control and far-reaching authority over all the earth for a prescribed period of time (forty-two months). His worship will be *enforced by the death penalty*. God's holy people *will* ultimately, overcome this antichrist man of sin by their martyrdom, and *resurrection at the rapture*.

> **Rev. 12:11** And they overcame him by the blood of the Lamb, and by the word of their testimony; and they loved not their lives unto the death.

> **Rev. 14:8–9** And the third angel followed them, saying with a loud voice, If any man worship the beast and his image, and receive his mark in his forehead, or in his hand...

"*As many as would not* worship the image of the beast," in verse 15 above, makes it clear that man has a *choice* and is *not* forced—nevertheless, this "choice" may mean *death.*

17 And that no man might buy or sell, save he that had the mark, or the name of the beast, or the number of his name.

It will *not* be easy *to refuse* the very identifier (mark), which is a *false* promise to protect you and your loved ones from starvation, isolation, rejection, and brutality. The *false* prophet and the beast attempt to hijack man's allegiance from God to serve their own sham government. They lure men to go after *worldly prizes* like approval, power, pleasure, and money. The self-deceived want to believe this *idolatrous substitute for God* will somehow save them, and provide for their needs. *The reality is that it will condemn them.* The beast's *system* is *antagonistic* to God and is *faithless* of His provisions.

Many who live their everyday lives *carelessly distant from God,* will *subtly* be enticed *in their minds,* to "*Go ahead and take the government-mandated mark.*" The mark *may* be called something noble, like "contact tracing" for safety, but it will *not be called* "the mark of the beast." *One's submission to the mandated "mark" will start in the heart that knows not God, even before a physical mark is ever accepted.* Renew your mind in Christ by knowing the Word of God.

Fear will reign over faith in all those who have *neglected* to have a *relationship* with God, their Creator. God wants us to trust and fear *Him alone.*

Matthew 10:28 And fear not them which kill the body, but are not able to kill the soul: but rather fear him which is able to destroy both soul and body in hell.

Refusing the offer of provision and protection from the deceptive "man of sin," and *instead* practicing faithfulness *to God* will mean the loss of friends, relatives, close family, and even your very home or *life*. This decision will place any "resister" in the category of *an enemy of the people*, a social misfit, and a "disease" to be *eradicated*.

It is sobering to claim that *the mark of allegiance* is *not* a *forced* mark, when in actuality, refusal to take it is a promissory *death* sentence. That decision will have to be made by God's people when the time comes. *No faithful, genuine child of God will take the mark, so don't worry that you will. If you know that you know you are a genuine believer and follower of Jesus Christ, God will keep you.*

18 Here is wisdom. Let him that hath understanding count the number of the beast: for it is the number of a man; and his number is Six hundred threescore and six.

The symbolical number 666 is *earthly* and falls short of what is heavenly. Seven is the symbolic number of perfection, and pertaining to God. *The number 666 represents a deceptive, cunning man and system, that is faithless and earthly all the way.* Don't take *any* mark of *compliance and allegiance,* in your body, if you are threatened with losing human rights should you *not* take it. .

God is *able* to keep His own people. Don't fear that you will "cave in" to the Antichrist if you are staying close to God. Trust your Heavenly Father with genuine and unwavering faith.

The beast will one day attempt to force all people to receive a *mark* on or in their bodies. He will *command* submission to him, as if he is a god. Those who refuse to honor and revere him, or even worship him, and refuse to take his *mark* will lose the right to buy and sell. They will essentially be locked down or imprisoned. Whether the *mark* is an implanted chip, a tracker, a tattoo, or some other symbol, it will represent allegiance and trust in the man of sin, as opposed to unrelenting faith in our all-loving God. To take the beast's *mark* will eternally doom the one who receives it.

CHAPTER 18

Loud Angelic Instructions and Harvest Operations

Revelation 14

1 And I looked, and, lo, a Lamb stood on the mount Zion, and with him an hundred forty *and* four thousand, having his Father's name written in their foreheads.

2 And I heard a voice from heaven, as the voice of many waters, and as the voice of a great thunder: and I heard the voice of harpers harping with their harps:

3 And they sung as it were a new song before the throne, and before the four beasts, and the elders: and no man could learn that song but the hundred *and* forty *and* four thousand, which were redeemed from the earth.

This song of the redeemed, those who comprise the figurative 144,000, *cannot* be known by the lost. The joy of the Lord is *our* strength and song.

4 These are they which were not defiled with women; for they are virgins. These are they which follow the Lamb whithersoever he goeth.

These were redeemed from among men, *being* the firstfruits unto God and to the Lamb.

144,000 is a symbolic number. This large company of redeemed *Jewish and Christian believers* are those who have proved themselves *faithful to God.* They have suffered persecution in order to voluntarily separate themselves from the world, while in the world. 12 ×12 × 1,000 = 144,000. This is a representation of the thousands of *both* "branches" (Jews and Christians) in God's complete Church. This is apocalyptic language signifying *all* of God's faithful and true witnesses. They are *as* "virgin brides" to the bridegroom, our Lord Jesus Christ. Their "claim to fame" in this passage (virgins) is *not* about them literally being men who have avoided sexual relationships with women.

5 And in their mouth was found no guile: for they are without fault before the throne of God.

They have "no guile" because they have a Savior who took away *all* their sin.

6 And I saw another angel fly in the midst of heaven, having the everlasting gospel to preach unto them that dwell on the earth, and to every nation, and kindred, and tongue, and people,
7 Saying with a loud voice, Fear God, and give glory to him; for the hour of his judgment is come: and worship him that made heaven, and earth, and the sea, and the fountains of waters.

God is still offering rebellious mankind warnings and instruction. Redemption is still available. This angel is flying through the sky and loudly shouting final warnings and pleas to all sinners. Again, I am struggling with the temptation to make the symbolic literal. Well, anyway, God is *still* sending out *strong* warnings to sinners at this point in the end of days. Perhaps these *are* real, literal angels flying through the air and shouting warnings. I hope so.

8 And there followed another angel, saying, Babylon is fallen, is fallen, that great city, because she made all nations drink of the wine of the wrath of her fornication.
9 And the third angel followed them, saying with a loud voice, If any man worship the beast and his image, and receive *his* mark in his forehead, or in his hand,
10 The same shall drink of the wine of the wrath of God, which is poured out without mixture into the cup of his indignation; and he shall be tormented with fire and brimstone in the presence of the holy angels, and in the presence of the Lamb:
11 And the smoke of their torment ascendeth up for ever and ever: and they have no rest day nor night, who worship the beast and his image, and whosoever receiveth the mark of his name.

Now *three* angels are flying through the sky and warning sinners. I should say, that *figuratively* speaking, *God is multiplying and intensifying his last calls and warnings.*

We also need to warn people. This "day" will soon be upon us. We must overcome our fear of man, and any fear of rejection, and just *find a way* to witness truth to the lost.

12 Here is the patience of the saints: here *are* they that keep the commandments of God, and the faith of Jesus.

This is *still* a redemptive period of tribulation. John has brought us to the very doorstep of the harvest of the earth, and God is dispatching *clear, loud* warnings to every nation, kindred, tongue, and people. He warns of the consequences of worshipping the beast and receiving his mark. And yet, already today, the news tells us that people are *currently*, readily, taking a man-made "mark" in order to do their earthly, economic business. To take a *physical mark,* might involve an injection. Be on high alert if the mandates to take any sort of mark get stronger, and the penalties for resisting, stiffer. *No one* can afford to make a wrong decision, when the Antichrist's *mark* is a ticket to eternal doom. I don't think it is here yet, but certainly it is right around the corner. We are in the times of a "test run."

The "mark" is already in the "forehead," or the *mind and heart,* whenever one accepts a *physical* mark. *The right hand is symbolic.* The mark is simply accepted *somewhere in the body,* and *cannot* be removed without the removal of the body part where it is implanted.

13 And I heard a voice from heaven saying unto me, Write, Blessed *are* the dead which die in the Lord from henceforth: Yea, saith the Spirit, that they may rest from their labours; and their works do follow them.

This passive voice is the voice of God. This passage shows that there are still people who are blessed of God on earth and labor for the cause of Christ.

14 And I looked, and behold a white cloud, and upon the cloud *one* sat like unto the Son of man, having on his head a golden crown, and in his hand a sharp sickle.

Jesus is ready to do some reaping!

15 And another angel came out of the temple, crying with a loud voice to him that sat on the cloud, Thrust in thy sickle, and reap: for the time is come for thee to reap; for the harvest of the earth is ripe. **16** And he that sat on the cloud thrust in his sickle on the earth; and the earth was reaped.

17 And another angel came out of the temple which is in heaven, he also having a sharp sickle.

18 And another angel came out from the altar, which had power over fire; and cried with a loud cry to him that had the sharp sickle, saying, Thrust in thy sharp sickle, and gather the clusters of the vine of the earth; for her grapes are fully ripe.

This is the day when the *tares,* those who have *refused* the mercy of God, will be harvested and cast into hell after their final conflict with God at the battle of Armageddon. The wheat and tares are separated at this time. This happens at the last trumpet.

19 And the angel thrust in his sickle into the earth, and gathered the vine of the earth, and cast *it* into the great winepress of the wrath of God. **20** And the winepress was trodden without the city, and blood came out of the winepress, even unto the horse bridles, by the space of a thousand *and* six hundred furlongs.

CHAPTER 19

Preparation for God's Wrath

Revelation 15

1 And I saw another sign in heaven, great and marvelous, seven angels having the seven last plagues; for in them is filled up the wrath of God.

J ohn is saying, "And I *also* saw this." He is *not* telling a chronological story that goes like, "And *next* this happened and then that happened." Revelation 15 is another *interlude*.

To give you an example, try to tell the story of a volcanic eruption. First, you might tell about the eruption itself, then the fire, then the people fleeing, then what their thoughts are, then what the officials in town are doing behind the scenes. Next, you might tell about the homes that were destroyed and the carnage and the survivors and finally, the end. You necessarily tell it in *separate narratives,* even though it was all happening simultaneously as one big event. That is the way John reported the seal and trumpet judgments . They are one big event, *taking place over a complete and perfect period of time,* (represented by a symbolic three and a half years) in God's purview and control.

But *the last seven judgments*, which are *the bowl judgments*, (also called vial judgments) are different. God's people, the faithful followers of Jesus Christ, *will not be here on earth for these judgments*. For that reason, I will not expound on the interpretation of these symbolic details. It won't matter how much detail we fully grasp about these judgments if *we are rescued from them*. The *most* important thing is that we faithfully cling to the Savior, *escape* them, and *warn* sinners to *flee the wrath of God* which is coming.

2 And I saw as it were a sea of glass mingled with fire: and them that had gotten the victory over the beast, and over his image, and over his mark, *and* over the number of his name, stand on the sea of glass, having the harps of God.

3 And they sing the song of Moses the servant of God, and the song of the Lamb, saying, Great and marvelous *are* thy works, Lord God Almighty; just and true *are* thy ways, thou King of saints.

4 Who shall not fear thee, O Lord, and glorify thy name? for *thou* only *art* holy: for all nations shall come and worship before thee; for thy judgments are made manifest.

5 And after that I looked, and behold, the temple of the tabernacle of the testimony in heaven was opened:

6 And the seven angels came out of the temple, having the seven plagues, clothed in pure and white linen, and having their breasts girded with golden girdles.

7 And one of the four beasts gave unto the seven angels seven golden vials full of the wrath of God, who liveth for ever and ever.

8 And the temple was filled with smoke from the glory of God, and from his power; and no man was able to enter into the temple, till the seven plagues of the seven angels were fulfilled.

The true Church, or the saints, will *not* be exposed to *any* of these events because the Church will have been raptured and will not be on earth. Revelation 16 is God's *wrath* on all the hardened, God-forsaking *rebels* who have refused to repent and turn to God. These rebels have refused *every* invitation to receive God's grace and mercy. Isn't that sad? We probably all know many of these people right now.

CHAPTER 20

Seven Vials of Wrath— It Is Done!

Revelation 16

1 And I heard a great voice out of the temple saying to the seven angels, Go your ways, and pour out the vials of the wrath of God upon the earth.

2 And the first went, and poured out his vial upon the earth; and there fell a noisome and grievous sore upon the men which had the mark of the beast, and *upon* them which worshipped his image.

3 And the second angel poured out his vial upon the sea; and it became as the blood of a dead *man:* and every living soul died in the sea.

4 And the third angel poured out his vial upon the rivers and fountains of waters; and they became blood.

5 And I heard the angel of the waters say, Thou art righteous, O Lord, which art, and wast, and shalt be, because thou hast judged thus.

6 For they have shed the blood of saints and prophets, and thou hast given them blood to drink; for they are worthy.

7 And I heard another out of the altar say, Even so, Lord God Almighty, true and righteous *are* thy judgments.

8 And the fourth angel poured out his vial upon the sun; and power was given unto him to scorch men with fire.

9 And men were scorched with great heat, and blasphemed the name of God, which hath power over these plagues: and they repented not to give him glory.

10 And the fifth angel poured out his vial upon the seat of the beast; and his kingdom was full of darkness; and they gnawed their tongues for pain,

11 And blasphemed the God of heaven because of their pains and their sores, and repented not of their deeds.

12 And the sixth angel poured out his vial upon the great river Euphrates; and the water thereof was dried up, that the way of the kings of the east might be prepared.

13 And I saw three unclean spirits like frogs *come* out of the mouth of the dragon, and out of the mouth of the beast, and out of the mouth of the false prophet.

14 For they are the spirits of devils, working miracles, *which* go forth unto the kings of the earth and of the whole world, to gather them to the battle of that great day of God Almighty.

The Church is not *of* the earth or *of* the world. We are citizens *of heaven.*

15 Behold, I come as a thief. Blessed *is* he that watcheth, and keepeth his garments, lest he walk naked, and they see his shame.

16 And he gathered them together into a place called in the Hebrew tongue Armageddon.

17 And the seventh angel poured out his vial into the air; and there came a great voice out of the temple of heaven, from the throne, saying, It is done.

18 And there were voices, and thunders, and lightnings; and there was a great earthquake, such as was not since men were upon the earth, so mighty an earthquake, *and* so great.

19 And the great city was divided into three parts, and the cities of the nations fell: and great Babylon came in remembrance before God, to give unto her the cup of the wine of the fierceness of his wrath.

20 And every island fled away, and the mountains were not found.

21 And there fell upon men a great hail out of heaven, *every stone* about the weight of a talent: and men blasphemed God because of the plague of the hail; for the plague thereof was exceeding great.

Don't be confused. John just expressed his vision about God's wrath on all the earth-dwellers, which happens *immediately after the rapture* but in concert with this same great and dreadful day of the Lord.

Following this chapter, John, once again, will write about *past events* during another *parenthetical interlude*. Revelation 17 and 18 will go back to in time to fill in more information and details about the players and events *during the time of the seals and trumpets.* Some of the events that are detailed in Revelation 17 and 18 depict the *history* of Babylon the Great, the mother of harlots, and *some* of what John writes is not just about Babylon *in the very end*, but *in all the ages past*. Babylon is an *ancient* empire. *Revelation 17 and 18 are interludes* in the book of Revelation, with a climatic ending. In chapter 19, we will see the *reaction* of all who are *saved*, and then John says the marriage supper of the Lamb *is come*.

> **Revelation 19:1** And after these things I heard a great voice of much people in heaven, saying, Alleluia; Salvation, and glory, and honour, and power, unto the Lord our God:

207

> **Revelation 19:7** Let us be glad and rejoice, and give honour to him: for the marriage of the Lamb is come, and his wife hath made herself ready.

Revelation 17 is the chapter about Babylon. Babylon has always been a fascinating and mysterious entity for students of Bible prophecy, myself included. The Babylonian empire or system is not only a political and economic system in the world, it is a *counterfeit and compromised religious system. Babylon has been in the world since the fall of mankind in the Garden of Eden.*

Geographic Babylon was an ancient city of the famous ziggurat tower—known as the Tower of Babel, which was mankind's first great attempt at a worldwide dictatorial government, combined with mystical religion and military might. It was mankind's attempt to secure God's blessings *through human unity,* just like we see happening today with the cry for *unity* to accomplish peace on earth. The visible Church is uniting with those who have put aside doctrine and convictions, in order to be in harmony with the kingdoms *of man,* who *deceptively* seek peace *without the rule of God.*

The name Babylon relates to how God defeated this ancient and ungodly regime, by turning all intelligent speech into babbling, when He caused all the people to speak in separate unfamiliar languages *to destroy their unity.*

In the apocalyptic and prophetic book of Revelation, Babylon represents *all* of the previous evil empires in one *final empire.* Modern Babylon will eventually attempt to use its base of power to destroy Israel *and all* of God's true, spiritual children of Abraham, *both the redeemed Jews and Gentile Christians alike.*

Prophecies about Babylon are sometimes confusing because, depending on the biblical context and location in the Bible, they may refer to either the actual physical, geographical Babylon, or they may refer to the *modern* economic, and political *system, representative of* the original Babylonian empire. John the Revelator writes about the *modern-day Babylon regime or worldly system,* which will empower a single, immensely powerful leader, who is the Antichrist.

Since the beginning of his reign as "the god of this world," *Satan,* when he was cast out of heaven, has used all of his demonic forces to inspire continuous rebellion against God. He causes leaders to initiate and maintain conflicts between the world's many diverse people and nations. *His end-game plan is to deceive the nations, in order that he may one day come on the scene as a "man of peace" to unite the world against God, through a deceptive peace plan.*

The earth-dwellers who will support the Antichrist might consider themselves well-intentioned, but they will be deceived. They will not and cannot make right decisions in order to save their own flesh and souls because they will not embrace the truth. These earth-dwellers will be those who have not taken the time to know what the Word of God says. They will refuse to listen to truth-speakers or the witnesses of God's holy Word. They will make decisions based on fear of man, not God.

The Bible says, that not knowing the Scriptures, is the source of man's errors (Matt. 22:29). One must have a true knowledge and right understanding of the Scriptures in order to be in right relationship with God and in order to recognize deception and counterfeits. The earth-dwellers who primarily spend their lives on earth seeking approval, pleasure, power, riches, and merchandise will not comprehend what is happening because they choose to leave God out of their daily lives. They don't think they need too much of God. They don't want the conviction of God against their sin. They prefer darkness to light. So now they are deceived. Careless agnostics who ignore the witness of God in their everyday lives will not escape the delusion God sends them.

A new world order will soon arise. I believe it is already in formation. *It will be sold as, or appear to be* a system of peace and prosperity to unite all people through mandated, non-exclusive, religious *tolerance*, with a universal deity, and in accordance with international agreements and laws. This new world order will be directed and administered by a world court, and under global organizations that answer to one man, the Antichrist. He won't be called this, of course. Initially, he will appear as an *ordinary*, talented man. The people of the nations will voluntarily submit to this prophesied antichrist *hero*, and place all their hope in him to mitigate and fix all of the global problems. The masses will surrender their God-ordained individual liberties in continuous small steps until they lose control of their daily lives and their eternal life as well.

CHAPTER 21

Unmasking the Details of Mystery Babylon

Revelation 17

1 And there came one of the seven angels which had the seven vials, and talked with me, saying unto me, Come hither; I will shew unto thee the judgment of the great whore that sitteth upon many waters:

Babylon has a name: "The Great Whore." She is a world-wide entity. Her national borders are "water." The water, also called the sea, symbolically refers to *many people*. It also may literally mean that Babylon has *ocean borders*. Babylon is later referred to as a *great city* in Revelation 18:10 and in 18:19, but Babylon is *anything but "great."* She is an *unfaithful whore*. The Great Whore has two faces. Babylon is her *secular, or political, face*. This is her *national* and *worldly position* in the earth. Her *spiritual face* is the face of the *harlot*. This is the face of the worldwide spiritually apostate Church.

Revelation 17 is a depiction of *the time of judgment* on the wicked *after* the Church has been rescued. That means the faithful Church will *not* be here for any of it. We are spared from the wrath of God. This chapter all relates to the unrighteous only, and the day of the Lord.

2 With whom the kings of the earth have committed fornication, and the inhabitants of the earth have been made drunk with the wine of her fornication.

The Great Whore has power and influence over world rulers. To gain positions of authority, many unscrupulous, political characters have *used* the *visible* Church in their rise to power. This is the "Church" in the "*outer* courtyard" who, when measured by God's plumbline is *not* found to be upright and genuine in following Jesus Christ. The apostate Church is without the Holy Spirit's "oil" in their "lamps" because they were either lazy and faithless pew-warmers, or they loved the world and failed to prepare to meet God.

3 So he carried me away in the spirit into the wilderness: and I saw a woman sit upon a scarlet coloured beast, full of names of blasphemy, having seven heads and ten horns.

The "woman" or the whore, in verse 3 is intimately related to the beast. The beast is "taking her for a ride." This is all figurative. She is riding on top, initially, and appears to be in control, but Revelation 17:16 shows the beast making her desolate, eating her flesh, and burning her with fire. The spiritual take-away is that *the beast will use the apostate church to rise to power.* The Antichrist will court *the visible Church* in his rise to power. *Ingenuine* believers and all earth-dwellers will believe in him. They will believe in themselves. Once this Christ-imposter beast consolidates his power, he no longer needs the Church and will seek to legally destroy *all* religiosity, and attempt to lock the true God completely out of life itself. Babylon seeks not just to get *rid* of God but attempts to *replace* God. The antichrist and his system are *deified*. Allegiance to the ruler, Antichrist (the first beast), will be required.

4 And the woman was arrayed in purple and scarlet colour, and decked with gold and precious stones and pearls, having a golden cup in her hand full of abominations and filthiness of her fornication:

This "woman," remember, is a harlot. This is not the same "woman" we encountered in Revelation 12, which represents the true Church. *This* woman is a *whore* who represents the *false*, compromised religious system. The pride, wealthiness and attractiveness of this *false religious system* are abominable to God.

Many students of Bible prophecy have noted that purple and scarlet are the traditional colors of the Roman Catholic Church, which is the major religion of *America*. How many times do we see the priests of the Catholic Church holding up their *golden cup* of communion? In verse four, this is a *symbolic* golden cup that is full of secret sins, abominations, filthiness, and fornication of unholy, imposters and ingenuine, deceived *religious people*.

Few people, Catholics included, read *papal encyclicals* and *Vatican documents*. But if they did, they would see the leader of the Catholic Church, *Pope Francis, is actively and deliberately advancing the goals of a one-world government and one-world religion* with his cloaked and deceitful language of brotherly love, *in his disturbing and apostate encyclicals*. He is setting the table for the persecution of all genuine Christians who remain faithful to *the original gospel of the inerrant, holy Bible.*

5 And upon her forehead *was* a name written, MYSTERY, BABYLON THE GREAT, THE MOTHER OF HARLOTS AND ABOMINATIONS OF THE EARTH.

This mystery is not in the sense of a riddle, but mystery because it is *hidden* until God reveals it. Babylon first shows up in the Bible in Genesis 11. It was a powerful empire that came up after the great flood of Noah's day. This empire, originally ruled by Nimrod, was characterized by rebellion, self-centeredness, confusion, witchcraft, divination, pride, a Jezebel spirit, lust for power, prosperity, deification of man, and exchanging the truth of God for lies. *The spirit of Babylon is self-rule, apart from God.*

Israel was to be God's exclusive bride, or wife, and was to be a light to the rest of the world, for God's blessings through her. She was to give God her exclusive love. But Israel went a *whoring* after another lover, namely *America.* (Ezek. 16:32–33). She cheated on God, her *true* lover, with America, Babylon.

6 And I saw the woman drunken with the blood of the saints, and with the blood of the martyrs of Jesus: and when I saw her, I wondered with great admiration.

The blood of many Christian martyrs stain the hands of the harlot. False religious systems have killed many Christians over the ages. One of America's largest religious institutions, the Roman Catholic Church, *has blood-stained hands* in the deaths of thousands and thousands of Christian martyrs.

During the time of great tribulation on earth, the harlot will martyr *many more Christians.* The harlot, *inclusive of all apostate religion,* is hostile to the *true* followers of Jesus Christ. Just try to witness *truth,* right out of the Holy Bible, to *any* "believers" in compromised churches, or even to your own lukewarm family members for that matter, and you will see. *They will not have it.* They will not attempt *any genuine dialogue to seek truth.*

7 And the angel said unto me, Wherefore didst thou marvel? I will tell thee the mystery of the woman, and of the beast that carrieth her, which hath the seven heads and ten horns.

John writes that initially, the beast tolerates and "carries" the organized, visible, religious systems for his own gain. Then John informs that the apostate church, which is carried by the beast, has seven heads and ten horns. John explains that the seven heads are *seven mountains, which represent nations.* The horns *represent rulers.* These are the seven rulers (horns) of Daniel 7:20, in which Daniel describes a beast with ten horns, and then three horns fell, (or were plucked up by the roots—Dan. 7:8) leaving seven.

> **Daniel 7:3-8** And four great beasts came up from the sea, diverse one from another. The first *was* like a **lion**, and had eagle's wings: I beheld till the wings thereof were plucked, and it was lifted up from the earth, and made stand upon the feet as a man, and a man's heart was given to it. And behold another beast, a second, like to a **bear**, and it raised up itself on one side, and *it had* three ribs in the mouth of it between the teeth of it: and they said thus unto it, Arise, devour much flesh. After this I beheld, and lo another, like a **leopard**, which had upon the back of it four wings of a fowl;

the beast had also four heads; and dominion was given to it. After this I saw in the night visions, and behold a **fourth beast, dreadful and terrible**, and strong exceedingly; and it had great iron teeth: it devoured and brake in pieces, and stamped the residue with the feet of it: and it *was* **diverse from all the beasts that** *were* **before it; and it** **had ten horns.** I considered the horns, and, behold, **there came up among them another little horn,** before whom there were **three of the first horns plucked up by the roots**: and, behold, in this horn *were* eyes like the eyes of man, and a mouth speaking great things.

Daniel 7:24-25 And the **ten horns** out of this kingdom *are* **ten kings** *that* **shall arise**: and **another shall rise after them;** and he shall be diverse from the first, and **he shall subdue three kings.** And he shall speak *great* words against the most High, and **shall wear out the saints of the most High,** and think to change times and laws: and **they shall be given into his hand until a time and times and the dividing of time.**

The modern-day "*beast*" of Revelation, and of Daniel's vision, is a picture of *one* of the kings, or rulers, who **arose out of**, and is an *extension of, the fourth beast's ten horns.* This *little horn* rises up, uproots, and shucks off three horns, or ruling kings. America, in her inception, shucked off England, France, and Spain. Hmmmmm!

8 The beast that thou sawest was, and is not; and shall ascend out of the bottomless pit, and go into perdition: and they that dwell on the earth shall wonder, whose names were not written in the book of life from the foundation of the world, when they behold the beast that was, and is not, and yet is.

9 And here *is* the mind which hath wisdom. The seven heads are seven mountains, on which the woman sitteth.
10 And there are seven kings: five are fallen, and one is, *and* the other is not yet come; and when he cometh, he must continue a short space.

In verse 10, John the Revelator saw five empires that *had already fallen* before his day. Those empires were Egypt, Assyria, Babylon, Medo-Persia, and Greece. Those are the five beasts that *had already fallen.* John would say that the Roman empire *is* in power in his day. That would make the Roman empire the sixth beast of his vision. The beast that John said would rise up in the future and give birth to *the eighth,* final antichrist beast *was not* the empire ruling in John's day. This eighth beast, John said, was a *previous* empire, and that is *revived Babylon.*

11 And the beast that was, and is not, even he is the eighth, and is of the seven, and goeth into perdition.
12 And the ten horns which thou sawest are ten kings, which have received no kingdom as yet; but receive power as kings one hour with the beast.

One hour is symbolic of a short time.

13 These have one mind, and shall give their power and strength unto the beast.
14 These shall make war with the Lamb, and the Lamb shall over-come them: for he is Lord of lords, and King of kings: and they that are with him *are* called, and chosen, and faithful.

Did you hear that? The *Lamb* is King of kings and Lord of lords. Bet you already knew that.

15 And he saith unto me, The waters which thou sawest, where the whore sitteth, are peoples, and multitudes, and nations, and tongues. 16 And the ten horns which thou sawest upon the beast, these shall hate the whore, and shall make her desolate and naked, and shall eat her flesh, and burn her with fire. 17 For God hath put in their hearts to fulfil his will, and to agree, and give their kingdom unto the beast, until the words of God shall be fulfilled. 18 And the woman which thou sawest is that great city, which reigneth over the kings of the earth.

The United Nations in New York City, and Rome alike, court the rulers of the world, but only *one* nation in the world today fits *all the descriptions* of Babylon the Great. *Revelation 18* and *Jeremiah 50 and 51* give an abundance of clear information to identify *this end-time nation* that produces the antichrist. *This is one nation,* and it is *the United States.* Take the time to read Jeremiah 50 and 51. Let's look at some of the evidence together.

Slowly, over the decades, America has been transforming into a godless nation. The numbers of Satanists, Wiccans, Atheists, New-Agers, God-haters, agnostics, Muslims, Hindus, and every form of cult religion are increasing in America each year. Pornography, homosexuality, abortion, perversions, human-trafficking, idolatry, violence, divorce, the breakup of the traditional family, alcohol and drug abuse, criminal activity, debauchery, and the profaning of God's name are all *commonplace* in American society. On TV and in the movies, these sins are *the norm. The love of money* and *self-love* occupy people's hearts more than the love of God. America actually *celebrates* homosexuality, abortion, and *every form of perversion.* Judges now pander to atheists and God-*haters.* Mothers by the hundreds of thousands *kill* their in-utero *babies,* and some of our government leaders openly and publicly celebrate their decisions. Mothers and fathers parade in the streets and scream that it is their right to end the lives of their preborn *babies* so they can get on with their lives without the inconvenience and expense of raising a child.

Enough evidence exists for me to conclude, without reservation, that America has been *deceived* into believing that her *roots* are exclusively Judeo-Christian. But there really is *no* "Christian nation" on earth that is under God's authority, not even America. Ungodly, occult, masonic, and gnostic philosophies have been incorporated into the very fabric and foundation of our nation *from its inception.* Our monuments, paintings, symbols, plaques, and other works of art, especially in government places and on public lands, frequently glorify ancient false gods and goddesses, the occult, and even Satan, but it is *rare* if you will ever see any that glorify Jesus Christ.

> **Matthew 7:18** A good tree cannot bring forth evil fruit, neither can a corrupt tree bring forth good fruit.

But what *specifically,* makes this *Mystery Babylon the Great,* none other than the United States of America? After all, the sins of America seem quite universal these days. Well, I'm glad you asked because I would like to share with you some *very specific indicators* of why it is, without a doubt, America.

CHAPTER 22

Babylon Forever the Loser

Revelation 18

1 And after these things I saw another angel come down from heaven, having great power; and the earth was lightened with his glory. 2 And he cried mightily with a strong voice, saying, Babylon the great is fallen, is fallen, and is become the habitation of devils, and the hold of every foul spirit, and a cage of every unclean and hateful bird.

B abylon, at one time, was great in the eyes of the world. She was extremely wealthy, and morally "riding high," but she is now *a stronghold of demons.* America is a land of religious confusion and spiritual harlotry. The organized Church incorporates an ecumenical and social gospel into their religious doctrines and dogmas. They have watered down the true gospel, minimized sin, and incorporated man's traditions as *equal to* the written Word of God. Saving the earth, loving without judging, and "taking America back" are modern-day mantras of the visible Church in America.

The foul spirits of America are sexual perversion, abortion, violence, infidelity, the destruction of the family, pride, greed, self-love, deceitfulness, and idolatry. *These sins are incorporated into every facet of our society, and sadly, prevalent in the visible Church.* America prides herself in incorporating and legislating into society every aberrant, immoral, and deviant lifestyle and practice, under the guise of freedom and "winning."

3 For all nations have drunk of the wine of the wrath of her fornication, and the kings of the earth have committed fornication with her, and the merchants of the earth are waxed rich through the abundance of her delicacies.

America is the most extravagant consumer nation in the world. The people have been corrupted to love and trust in earthly riches. God has been dethroned for money. Families are falling apart as moms and dads work overtime to upgrade their lifestyle, desiring to be the object of envy to their friends. The pride of life has people clamoring to be noticed and applauded. They love themselves and have a lust for more of the best, the newest, and the finest of everything. Babylon is trapped in a net of sinfulness through her pride, greed, vanity, homosexuality and perversions, faithlessness, lukewarmness, self-centeredness, deceptions and lies, lusts, crime, abortion, murders, hatefulness, and godless ambitions. Our churches in America are laughing and joyful when we should be in great heaviness of heart for the sinful condition of our people.

Even the Church's conversations in the many Sunday school rooms and foyers has slidden to nothing more than marketplace chatter, devoid of an interest in the things of God. Christian fellowship in the Church is important, but it ceases to be true Christian fellowship when it is not Christ-centered. It is simply "fellowship." All Christian fellowshipping in a church setting should attempt to support believers in their walk of faith, holiness, service, and steadfastness to a *holy* God. Many churches have replaced godly fellowshipping with simple amusements and entertainment.

The materialistic Church in America wants to serve two masters, God and money, but scripture warns that this is not possible. The Church in America does not look much different than the unclean and hateful birds in Revelation 18:2. Congregants attend services, sway to the music, raise their hands when they are moved by emotions, and leave *untouched*. They exit the building still filled with selfish desires, self-love, materialistic conquests, false religion, greed, anger, pride, ungratefulness, disrespectfulness, immoral thoughts, lust, conceit, unforgiveness, laziness, and immoral dress. They exit their weekly church services and go home to plop on their couches and consume irreverent entertainment. They carelessly live like the world, unaware of God's imminent, impending judgment on all sinners. Many continue to be promiscuous, unrestrained, undisciplined, indecent, extravagant, disrespectful of human life, and utterly corrupt. *I'm talking about churchgoers.*

Evangelism has been replaced with causes that demand social action to improve the conditions of the earth. Good politics and good government are wedded with the gospel in our pulpits to save the nation from our greatest perceived enemies: communism and socialism. (In reality, we need to be about eternal souls being saved.) The importance of good secular government is raised above Christian virtue and prayer to save the nation from God's impending judgment. Politics is raised over a relationship with the King Omnipotent, and over prayer and praise to God.

Jesus warned the churches that in the last days, much of the Church would be spiritually bankrupt and lukewarm. Our watchmen today are not weeping but are seeking to empower men to take over the reins of government and legislate righteousness. The Church is yearning to fix the beast's godless system of tyranny, forgetting that we are primarily to work on building God's eternal kingdom. *Our main commission does not change, no matter who is in power.*

The definition of Christianity in America has been subtly changed. To maintain the interest and support of the congregants, Church leaders are teaching their members to "take back America" and "Christianize" the world. Many of our churches teach a sugar-coated gospel, that *"God loves you just the way you are, and He has a wonderful plan for your life,* however it is." This gospel fills the pews with unregenerate rebels who cannot see the need to change.

America, and not excluding the visible Church, is so materialistic and self-loving that her primary interest is in maintaining and increasing her material wealth. Americans can never have enough stuff, especially the novel and the delicacies. On foreign shores, children and slave labor forces work overtime in factories to manufacture and assemble merchandise for Americans to consume. Our greed is their meal ticket.

4 And I heard another voice from heaven, saying, Come out of her, my people, that ye be not partakers of her sins, and that ye receive not of her plagues.

God pleads with his own people, "Stop this nonsense. Don't live like the rest of the world, for the *things* of this world are passing away. Forsake your *idolatry* and turn back to Me. I am the *only* one who can protect you from the judgments that are *soon* coming to destroy this greedy, immoral, prideful, and heathenistic harlot and the world of sin."

> **Joel 2:12–13** And rend your heart, and not your garments, and turn unto the LORD your God: for he *is* gracious and merciful, slow to anger, and of great kindness, and repenteth him of the evil.

> "There is no suffering for any class of God's people in any age like the sufferings of those who remain faithful to God during the reign of the Antichrist. Here, at this particular time and juncture, is the patience or endurance of them that keep the commandments of God and the faith of Jesus. To come out of Babylon, and to stand aloof from its horrible harlotries, is a costly thing."[6]

5 For her sins have reached unto heaven, and God hath remembered her iniquities.

God's standards are absolute. What was carved on two tablets of stone in the Old Testament, is still *the same* today. Sin then is sin now.

Many in the visible Church, like the earth-dwellers, are going about their daily lives as if nothing is going to happen. We are guilty of forgetting that *this earth is not our permanent home.* We are just *foreigners* here, passing through. We are charged by the Word of God to live our lives for *God's* mission, seeking to multiply the family of God through faithful witnessing and uncompromised lives. But we get so wrapped up with our families and friends and our *carnal desires* that *we* can be guilty of seeking pleasure more than we seek God.

Many Christians are pleasure-lovers, looking to be amused by the best of everything that money can buy. We are guilty of coveting the best vehicles, homes, furnishings, vacations, foods, delicacies, adornments, and fashion. The Church joins the pleasure-seeking crowds into sports arenas, concerts, and amusement parks, often taking dozens of pictures to post in social media accounts for virtual friends to envy. (I am not saying it is wrong to enjoy life. It is okay, as long as our amusements don't take us to a place of *forgetting* God and God's mission.) The Church is guilty of being amused by immoral characters on television and in movies. The Church is guilty of dressing sexy in tight, sheer, and minimal clothing designed to incite lust. The Church is guilty of loving the music of the world, that pumps out lyrics of sex and drugs and rock and roll. The Church is guilty of not separating themselves from the world and its ways. Without repentance, in order to receive God's grace and clemency, we would be so guilty and doomed. God, help us to come out of Babylon.

6 Reward her even as she rewarded you, and double unto her double according to her works: in the cup which she hath filled fill to her double.
7 How much she hath glorified herself, and lived deliciously, so much torment and sorrow give her: for she saith in her heart, I sit a queen, and am no widow, and shall see no sorrow.
8 Therefore shall her plagues come in one day, death, and mourning, and famine; and she shall be utterly burned with fire: for strong *is* the Lord God who judgeth her.

America will one day be overwhelmed with disease, virus, death, food shortages, floods, and fires burning out of control. It sounds like today's headlines. These judgments are ongoing, even today, but they will *increase*. They will rise to the level of God's unbridled wrath *after the rapture*. God's plan is holy, just, and righteous, and we don't fully understand everything now. But babies and innocents will be out of here, along with the saints. Have faith that God cares more than you and I do, and He will *not* allow the innocent to suffer his wrath.

9 And the kings of the earth, who have committed fornication and lived deliciously with her, shall bewail her, and lament for her, when they shall see the smoke of her burning,
10 Standing afar off for the fear of her torment, saying, Alas, alas, that great city Babylon, that mighty city. for in one hour is thy judgment come.
11 And the merchants of the earth shall weep and mourn over her; for no man buyeth their merchandise any more:
12 The merchandise of gold, and silver, and precious stones, and of pearls, and fine linen, and purple, and silk, and scarlet, and all thyine wood, and all manner vessels of ivory, and all manner vessels of most precious wood, and of brass, and iron, and marble,
13 And cinnamon, and odours, and ointments, and frankincense, and wine, and oil, and fine flour, and wheat, and beasts, and sheep, and horses, and chariots, and slaves, and souls of men.
14 And the fruits that thy soul lusted after are departed from thee, and all things which were dainty and goodly are departed from thee, and thou shalt find them no more at all.
15 The merchants of these things, which were made rich by her, shall stand afar off for the fear of her torment, weeping and wailing,

16 And saying, Alas, alas, that great city, that was clothed in fine linen, and purple, and scarlet, and decked with gold, and precious stones, and pearls.

17 For in one hour so great riches is come to nought. And every shipmaster, and all the company in ships, and sailors, and as many as trade by sea, stood afar off,

18 And cried when they saw the smoke of her burning, saying, What *city is* **like unto this great city.**

America burns. Babylon America is a multiple seaport nation. We are especially known for having the largest seaport in the Western world—New York City. In verse 15, the many foreign merchants on ships can't even pull into America's ports and deliver their merchandise for this great consumer nation because America is being destroyed right before their eyes.

America, the youngest ("hindermost") of the nations, is also known as "the hammer of the earth," the nation of "mingled people." In the days of Revelation 18, America will be known as a nation *once admired* for her beauty and Christian influence, her music, her international business, her space travel, and her leadership in the world. America will be great *no more.*

19 And they cast dust on their heads, and cried, weeping and wailing, saying, Alas, alas, that great city, wherein were made rich all that had ships in the sea by reason of her costliness. for in one hour is she made desolate.

This means it will happen *suddenly.* The word *city* is symbolic. *One hour* is figurative of a very short amount of time.

20 Rejoice over her, *thou* heaven, and *ye* holy apostles and prophets; for God hath avenged you on her.

21 And a mighty angel took up a stone like a great millstone, and cast *it* into the sea, saying, Thus with violence shall that great city Babylon be thrown down, and shall be found no more at all.

22 And the voice of harpers, and musicians, and of pipers, and trumpeters, shall be heard no more at all in thee; and no craftsman, of whatsoever craft *he be,* shall be found any more in thee; and the sound of a millstone shall be heard no more at all in thee;

23 And the light of a candle shall shine no more at all in thee; and the voice of the bridegroom and of the bride shall be heard no more at all in thee: for thy merchants were the great men of the earth; for by thy sorceries were all nations deceived.

> **Revelation 18:2** Then I heard another voice from heaven saying, "Come out of her, my people, lest you take part in her sins, lest you share in her plagues;

God does not want his people to *literally* depart from Babylon because we would have to depart from the earth to do so. God wants us to depart from *faithless* religion and disassociate ourselves from the spirit of Babylon. We are God's set-apart, *holy* people. We are not to adopt the sinful acts, attitudes, and motivations of the earth-dwellers. When we spend time in the company of sinful earth-dwellers, we are to be salt and light, and ambassadors of *our* King. We are *not* to be ashamed of who we are in Christ, and of who Christ is in us. We are God's body, his holy witnesses in the world.

24 And in her was found the blood of prophets, and of saints, and of all that were slain upon the earth.

CHAPTER 23

Two Different Suppers

Revelation 19

1 And after these things I heard a great voice of much people in heaven, saying, Alleluia; Salvation, and glory, and honour, and power, unto the Lord our God:

2 For true and righteous *are* his judgments: for he hath judged the great whore, which did corrupt the earth with her fornication, and hath avenged the blood of his servants at her hand.

Babylon has been judged with the *vial or bowl* judgments. The faithful Church has *no* part in this. Do you notice in 19:1 where the Church is? The Church was *rescued* and went up to heaven *before* God avenged Babylon for corrupting the entire earth and for killing God's righteous followers.

3 And again they said, Alleluia. And her smoke rose up for ever and ever.

4 And the four and twenty elders and the four beasts fell down and worshipped God that sat on the throne, saying, Amen; Alleluia.

5 And a voice came out of the throne, saying, Praise our God, all ye his servants, and ye that fear him, both small and great.

6 And I heard as it were the voice of a great multitude, and as the voice of many waters, and as the voice of mighty thunderings, saying, Alleluia: for the Lord God omnipotent reigneth.

7 Let us be glad and rejoice, and give honour to him: for the marriage of the Lamb is come, and his wife hath made herself ready.

8 And to her was granted that she should be arrayed in fine linen, clean and white: for the fine linen is the righteousness of saints.

9 And he saith unto me, Write, Blessed *are* they which are called unto the marriage supper of the Lamb. And he saith unto me, These are the true sayings of God.

This "marriage of the Lamb" and the "marriage supper of the Lamb" represent the scene *on the day of the Lord* where Jesus Christ's *full glory* is displayed. *The Lamb's wife/bride is His eternal body, made up of all the redeemed saints of every age. This is the complete Church.* John's visions present this revelation of *the Church as a bride* adorned.

This *bride of Christ* also represents the final Jerusalem, the heavenly home of every weary pilgrim who overcame the contamination and defilement of sin and evil. The apparel of the bride is the *imputed righteousness* of the loving bridegroom, Jesus Christ.

> **Isaiah 61:10** I will greatly rejoice in the LORD, my soul shall be joyful in my God; for he hath clothed me with the garments of salvation, he hath covered me with the robe of righteousness, as a bridegroom decketh himself with ornaments, and as a bride adorneth herself with her jewels.

The marriage of the Lamb in Revelation 19:7 is also figurative of the complete union between Christ and His faithful Church. This union is consummated on the last day when Satan has been overcome, and sin and death are *destroyed.* The marriage supper is symbolic of the joy and triumph in heaven when Satan is conquered, and Jesus Christ will possess His eternal kingdom with *His chosen family.*

> **Revelation 21:1-3** And I saw a new heaven and a new earth: for the first heaven and the first earth were passed away; and there was no more sea. And I John saw the holy city, new Jerusalem, coming down from God out of heaven, prepared as a bride adorned for her husband. And I heard a great voice out of heaven saying, Behold, the tabernacle of God *is* with men, and he will dwell with them, and they shall be his people, and God himself shall be with them, *and be* their God.

10 And I fell at his feet to worship him. And he said unto me, See *thou do it* not: I am thy fellow servant, and of thy brethren that have the testimony of Jesus: worship God: for the testimony of Jesus is the spirit of prophecy.
11 And I saw heaven opened, and behold a white horse; and he that sat upon him *was* called Faithful and True, and in righteousness he doth judge and make war.
12 His eyes *were* as a flame of fire, and on his head *were* many crowns; and he had a name written, that no man knew, but he himself.
13 And he *was* clothed with a vesture dipped in blood: and his name is called The Word of God.

That's Jesus Christ.

So many events are happening *in concert,* not on a horizontal timeline. When the Lord calls, "*Come up hither*" (at the sixth seal and seventh trumpet), graves open and saints rise up to the clouds to meet the Lord in the air. The Lord, on a figurative "white horse," and all of his armies in heaven, with all of the saints and martyrs who were in heaven, descend together as a cloud of witnesses. The body of Christ is transforming into eternal beings with glorified bodies. The "two witnesses," (both redeemed Jews and Gentiles) *and all the tribulation martyrs on earth, lying unburied on the streets, are coming alive again and are rising in the air to meet the Lord* (a shocking sight).

14 And the armies *which were* in heaven followed him upon white horses, clothed in fine linen, white and clean.

15 And out of his mouth goeth a sharp sword, that with it he should smite the nations: and he shall rule them with a rod of iron: and he treadeth the winepress of the fierceness and wrath of Almighty God.

16 And he hath on *his* vesture and on his thigh a name written, KING OF KINGS, AND LORD OF LORDS.

17 And I saw an angel standing in the sun; and he cried with a loud voice, saying to all the fowls that fly in the midst of heaven, Come and gather yourselves together unto the supper of the great God;

This "supper" is *not* the marriage supper of the Lamb.

18 That ye may eat the flesh of kings, and the flesh of captains, and the flesh of mighty men, and the flesh of horses, and of them that sit on them, and the flesh of all men, both free and bond, both small and great.

19 And I saw the beast, and the kings of the earth, and their armies, gathered together to make war against him that sat on the horse, and against his army.

20 And the beast was taken, and with him the false prophet that wrought miracles before him, with which he deceived them that had

received the mark of the beast, and them that worshipped his image. These both were cast alive into a lake of fire burning with brimstone. 21 And the remnant were slain with the sword of him that sat upon the horse, which *sword* proceeded out of his mouth: and all the fowls were filled with their flesh.

This is the remnant, of the rest of the earth-dwellers who have not yet been killed. God destroys them. This is the end of the war of Armageddon.

CHAPTER 24

Seven Years/One Thousand Years = The Perfect Number of Years

<u>**Revelation 20**</u>

1 And I saw an angel come down from heaven, having the key of the bottomless pit and a great chain in his hand.
2 And he laid hold on the dragon, that old serpent, which is the Devil, and Satan, and bound him a thousand years,

John sees this event in his apocalyptic vision, but this binding event happened when Satan was cast out of heaven "a thousand years ago." A thousand years is symbolic and stands for *a long and complete amount of time*, over all time since the beginning of creation.

3 And cast him into the bottomless pit, and shut him up, and set a seal upon him, that he should deceive the nations no more, till the thousand years should be fulfilled: and after that he must be loosed a little season.

After a long and complete amount of time, ("a thousand years") Satan will be *loosed* from the boundaries he currently operates under. He is *bound* but not completely. For a little while, in the last days, Satan will be loosed—off his leash. Can you believe, with all the wickedness in the world, that Satan has actually been bound? He still operates, but he *cannot* go beyond the *limits* God has set. God allows Satan to operate so mankind can be tested and choose to declare his allegiance or God's. People can *choose* to serve God and obey God, or rebel against him and choose lies, darkness, and sin.

4 And I saw thrones, and they sat upon them, and judgment was given unto them: and *I saw* the souls of them that were beheaded for the witness of Jesus, and for the word of God, and which had not worshipped the beast, neither his image, neither had received *his* mark upon their foreheads, or in their hands; and they lived and reigned with Christ a thousand years.

This passage relates to *the overcomers* in Revelation 12:11.

> **Revelation 12:11** And they overcame him (*the dragon*) by the blood of the Lamb, and by the word of their testimony; and they loved not their lives unto the death.

We are told nine times in Revelation that we must be overcomers to the end. Overcomers will one day eat of the Tree of Life. They will not be hurt by the second death. They will be fed hidden manna and clothed in white raiment. They will serve as pillars in the temple of God and will get to sit with Christ on his throne. Overcomers shall inherit all things as sons of God. Wow. What eternal privilege to be an overcomer to the end, even to the point of martyrdom.

This is a description of our position in Christ *in this life*. *We* are the ones who overcome evil. *Our* conduct in the world brings judgment to evildoers. Revelation 5:10 says, "And hast made **us** unto our God kings and priests: and we shall reign on the earth." We do not begin to live and reign with Christ only *after* the death of Christian martyrs in verse four. *Christians live and reign with Christ right now.* The children of God are free from the law of sin and death and are declared, "Not guilty." *We serve as righteous rulers, reigning with Christ, and defending the faith. We are kings and priests to God, and the devil does not have authority over us.*

5 But the rest of the dead lived not again until the thousand years were finished. This is the first resurrection.

The *first resurrection* John refers to in verse 5 is the resurrection he wrote of in verse 4 – those martyrs now living with Christ. This is the resurrection of the *overcomers*. The *first* resurrection is when believers awake from death to everlasting life. For believers, the *first resurrection* takes place over the span of this millennium, and is completed at the rapture.

6 Blessed and holy *is* he that hath part in the first resurrection: on such the second death hath no power, but they shall be priests of God and of Christ, and shall reign with him a thousand years.

God's end times deliverance, the first resurrection, -at the day of the Lord, is *immediately* followed by God's *wrath*, which comes with the vial, or bowl judgments, known as the great tribulation. The next verse is *not* to depict a chronological "next item on the agenda" event.

7 And when the <u>thousand years</u> are expired, Satan shall be <u>loosed</u> out of his prison,

In other words, when a long, and complete amount of time, in the history of the world, is up, Satan will be off the leash. *He is not going to be let out of hell after a literal thousand years after the last day, to tempt, try, kill, or destroy anyone or anything in God's kingdom. Death is destroyed on the day of the Lord.* It is false theology to think that God would need to give Satan a second shot at His creation once He has *already* conquered him and bound him forever. Satan is loosed at the end of the *long* time he has operated on earth, since the beginning of creation.

8 And shall go out to deceive the nations which are in the four quarters of the earth, Gog and Magog, to gather them together to battle: the number of whom *is* as the sand of the sea.

Satan has actually been *bound* since he was cast out of heaven. He must get permission from God, to operate. He has *no* power to overcome the people of God. *His strength is leashed.* Satan can only *tempt* mankind, and bring a measured amount of calamity and destruction. His God-ordained role is to separate real believers from pretenders. He and all his sorry followers are workers of iniquity, laboring to fulfill *God's* will for a period of time, which is a symbolic "thousand years."

Satan is *restricted* in this present age by God's omnipotent legal authority. His defeat is already assured. *For all righteous believers,* Satan is *bound* when we are submitted to Jesus Christ. He *must* flee from God's children when we *resist* him. Read James 4:7.

Righteous men are not under Satan's authority. He *cannot* prevent us from spreading the gospel, and he is not able to destroy the Church. All of the righteous saints of God are pardoned from sin by God's grace, and *securely remain* in Christ. *God* keeps us and imputes no sin on our account. Christ's death and resurrection *disarmed* Satan in his warfare against God's people.

> **Colossians 2:15** In this way, he disarmed the spiritual rulers and authorities. He shamed them publicly by his victory over them on the cross. **NLT**

Additional scripture verses relating to the restraint and binding of Satan and the fallen angels, are found in Luke 10:18–19, Matthew 12:28–29, 2 Peter 2:4, Jude 6, Ezekiel 28:12–19, and Isaiah 14.

Jesus came to earth to *destroy* the works of the devil. Read 1 John 3:7–9. Satan's power is *limited* and under the sovereign control of God *right now*, but Satan is by no means powerless. Satan is on a constant prowl seeking to devour the *unprotected*. He performs lying signs and wonders, and is a strong foe who has the ability to deceive all earth-dwellers who remain unreconciled to God. Read Revelation 13:14.

Satan has the ability to bring sickness, disease, and calamity upon people. He is doing God's *permissive* will for God's higher purposes.

> **Job 2:7** So Satan left the LORD's presence, and he struck Job with terrible boils from head to foot.

Luke 22:31 Simon, Simon, Satan has asked to sift each of you like wheat.

1 Corinthians 5:5 hand this *(sinful)* man over to Satan for the destruction of the flesh, so that his spirit may be saved on the day of the Lord.

Satan's plan is always to kill, steal, and destroy, but the Son of God was manifested to destroy these works (1 John 3:8).

James 4:7 Submit yourselves therefore to God. Resist the devil, and he will flee from you.

No excuse is accepted. *You* submit *yourself* to GOD. God *will* keep you from the devil's wiles according to His will for your life. Trust His plan and purposes. He will never fail you, and He will never get it wrong.

9 And they went up on the breadth of the earth, and compassed the camp of the saints about, and the beloved city: and fire came down from God out of heaven, and devoured them.

The main target and enemy of Satan is the Church, "the saints," and "Jerusalem," the beloved city. The common meaning for Jerusalem and the temple in Revelation is figurative of the true believers, the faithful followers of Jesus Christ.

The saints are cornered in verse 9. This is a cosmic clash—the *Gog and Magog* war, also called *Armageddon*, is also the time of *the rapture* of the "two witnesses" (the "144,000" who are *all* of God's redeemed people on earth, Jew and Gentile alike.) The earth-dwellers imagine they can now finally destroy the people who witness of Jesus Christ. The saints of God are cornered and surrounded, *but God intervenes.*

Jesus Christ will descend from heaven, accompanied by *all* his risen saints from earth and the intermediate heaven, with innumerable angels, and His vast armies in heaven. We will all *meet Him in the air* for this final cataclysmic event of justice. Some saints will be rising up, and some will be coming down with the Lord on this spectacular day. This is the long-awaited day in which Jesus Christ will be glorified in the saints. Judgment on every unregenerate rebel *from every age* occurs *immediately*, completely, and finally when the saints are all removed from the earth. Then all hell breaks loose. This will be nothing like the wrath of *man* or even *Satan.* This is the unbridled wrath and vengeance of a holy and offended *God.*

10 And the devil that deceived them was cast into the lake of fire and brimstone, where the beast and the false prophet *are*, and shall be tormented day and night for ever and ever.
11 And I saw a great white throne, and him that sat on it, from whose face the earth and the heaven fled away; and there was found no place for them.

The earth is burned up, and the heavens roll up. *It is over.* Judgment now commences.

12 And I saw the dead, small and great, stand before God; and the books were opened: and another book was opened, which is the book of life: and the dead were judged out of those things which were written in the books, according to their works.

The lost will become aware of every sin they ever committed. They will be aware of every time they closed their hearts and ears, and turned away from the Holy Spirit's pleading. They will be wrecked with shame and exposure as *the records of their lives* are opened and revealed to all.

> **Luke 12:2** For there is nothing covered, that shall not be revealed; neither hid, that shall not be known.

The lost will know that *by their own choice*, they rejected salvation. How eternally miserable they will be, forever recalling that the saints go off to a most beautiful place of peace, tranquility, love, comfort, and light that could have been theirs. Instead, *the wicked will face the irreversible consequences of their individual sins.* They will be punished according to their own sins.

> **2 Thessalonians 1:8–9** In flaming fire taking vengeance on them that know not God, and that obey not the gospel of our Lord Jesus Christ: Who shall be punished with everlasting destruction from the presence of the Lord, and from the glory of his power;

13 And the sea gave up the dead which were in it; and death and hell delivered up the dead which were in them: and they were judged every man according to their works.

Judgment of the wicked happens *immediately* following the end of the symbolic thousand years. God's justice will be promptly carried out against sinners, once the righteous are taken to heaven. Every action, word, thought, and motive of every sinner will be brought to light. The saints will see how fairly God deals with these lost rebels in his court of justice. Their sin is unpardoned *by their own choice.* Their sin will be weighed against the Word of God, and each will receive a **just** sentence of *eternal* punishment.

14 And death and hell were cast into the lake of fire. This is the second death.
15 And whosoever was not found written in the book of life was cast into the lake of fire.

The *last* enemy, *death,* shall be no more. The *devil,* and all those who refused God's grace, will remain in the pit of torment *forever.* Believe me, no one is getting out in a thousand years. That is most certainly a *wrong* interpretation.

CHAPTER 25

One Body Living with the Lamb

<u>Revelation 21</u>

1 And I saw a new heaven and a new earth: for the first heaven and the first earth were passed away; and there was no more sea.
2 And I John saw the holy city, new Jerusalem, coming down from God out of heaven, prepared as a bride adorned for her husband.

This verse identifies the "*holy city*" and the "*new Jerusalem*" as *God's people*, or "*as a bride*." The bride descends from heaven with Jesus at the time of the new heaven and earth.

3 And I heard a great voice out of heaven saying, Behold, the tabernacle of God *is* with men, and he will dwell with them, and they shall be his people, and God himself shall be with them, *and be* their God.

Jesus is called "*the tabernacle of God*." He will dwell with us in his perfect kingdom once the first earth has been burned up and is no more.

4 And God shall wipe away all tears from their eyes; and there shall be no more death, neither sorrow, nor crying, neither shall there be any more pain: for the former things are passed away.

5 And he that sat upon the throne said, Behold, I make all things new. And he said unto me, Write: for these words are true and faithful.

6 And he said unto me, It is done. I am Alpha and Omega, the beginning and the end. I will give unto him that is athirst of the fountain of the water of life freely.

7 He that overcometh shall inherit all things; and I will be his God, and he shall be my son.

If you have forgotten what *overcoming* entails, review Revelation 12:11.

8 But the fearful, and unbelieving, and the abominable, and murderers, and whoremongers, and sorcerers, and idolaters, and all liars, shall have their part in the lake which burneth with fire and brimstone: which is the second death.

The *fearful* are the *faithless* who don't know God and His Word *because they didn't want* to. Their sin of fear is listed among heinous sins. Without faith, it is *impossible* to please God.

9 And there came unto me one of the seven angels which had the seven vials full of the seven last plagues, and talked with me, saying, Come hither, I will shew thee the bride, the Lamb's wife.

10 And he carried me away in the spirit to a great and high mountain, and shewed me that great city, the holy Jerusalem, descending out of heaven from God,

John was summoned to go up with an angel to see "the bride," "the Lamb's wife." What he was shown is, "that great city, the holy Jerusalem descending out of heaven," just as we saw in Revelation 21:2. This "bride" is all the company of God's people who have died in every age and are awaiting their resurrected bodies and the great day of the Lord. These are redeemed Jews and Christians. They are *one* family of God. They are descending to meet their fellow servants and brethren who are rising to meet the Lord in the air.

11 Having the glory of God: and her light *was* like unto a stone most precious, even like a jasper stone, clear as crystal;

12 And had a wall great and high, *and* had twelve gates, and at the gates twelve angels, and names written thereon, which are *the names* of the twelve tribes of the children of Israel:

13 On the east three gates; on the north three gates; on the south three gates; and on the west three gates.

14 And the wall of the city had twelve foundations, and in them the names of the twelve apostles of the Lamb.

15 And he that talked with me had a golden reed to measure the city, and the gates thereof, and the wall thereof.

16 And the city lieth foursquare, and the length is as large as the breadth: and he measured the city with the reed, twelve thousand furlongs. The length and the breadth and the height of it are equal.

17 And he measured the wall thereof, an hundred *and* forty *and* four cubits, *according to* the measure of a man, that is, of the angel.

18 And the building of the wall of it was *of* jasper: and the city *was* pure gold, like unto clear glass.

19 And the foundations of the wall of the city *were* garnished with all manner of precious stones. The first foundation *was* jasper; the second, sapphire; the third, a chalcedony; the fourth, an emerald;

20 The fifth, sardonyx; the sixth, sardius; the seventh, chrysolite; the eighth, beryl; the ninth, a topaz; the tenth, a chrysoprasus; the eleventh, a jacinth; the twelfth, an amethyst.

The first symbolic foundation stone of the wall of the New Jerusalem is a jasper stone, probably a diamond. It is described in Revelation 21:11 as "clear as crystal." It symbolizes God's holiness and righteousness.

Nothing of this description of "the wall of the city" with twelve foundations, was intended to be *literally* understood. The rainbow of stones represents God's *mercy and grace,* like the rainbow in Genesis 9 that followed the flood.

21 And the twelve gates *were* twelve pearls; every several gate was of one pearl: and the street of the city *was* pure gold, as it were transparent glass.
22 And I saw NO temple therein: for the Lord God Almighty and the Lamb are the temple of it.

Jesus is the Tabernacle of God in verse 22 above. The Lamb is *one God* with the Lord God Almighty.

23 And the city had no need of the sun, neither of the moon, to shine in it: for the glory of God did lighten it, and the Lamb *is* the light thereof.
24 And the nations of them which are saved shall walk in the light of it: and the kings of the earth do bring their glory and honour into it.

These are the redeemed saints, kings and priests to God, in the *new* earth.

25 And the gates of it shall not be shut at all by day: for there shall be no night there.
26 And they shall bring the glory and honour of the nations into it.

27 And there shall in no wise enter into it any thing that defileth, neither whatsoever worketh abomination, or maketh a lie: but they which are written in the Lamb's book of life.

Only members of the *true spiritual Church* of Jesus Christ shall enter into heaven. The **genuinely** saved will renounce the devil and all his temptations, the pride of life, and the sinful lusts of the flesh, in order to keep God's holy Word and his commandments. *The saved seek God.* No one should expect eternal glory while living in sin.

God gives every man the same opportunity to call on Him and follow Him. All the lost will have had many invitations and opportunities to call on God. Those who do not, will be *without excuse* before God.

CHAPTER 26

Coming Soon!

<u>Revelation 22</u>

1 And he shewed me a pure river of water of life, clear as crystal, proceeding out of the throne of God and of the Lamb.

2 In the midst of the street of it, and on either side of the river, *was there* the tree of life, which bare twelve *manner of* fruits, *and* yielded her fruit every month: and the leaves of the tree *were* for the healing of the nations.

We first saw this Tree of Life in Genesis 2. God is bringing us back to the garden of Eden.

3 And there shall be no more curse: but the throne of God and of the Lamb shall be in it; and his servants shall serve him:

4 And they shall see his face; and his name *shall be* in their foreheads.

This is not to be taken literally. The saints have the mind of Christ.

1 Corinthians 2:16 For who hath known the mind of the Lord, that he may instruct him? But we have the mind of Christ.

5 And there shall be no night there; and they need no candle, neither light of the sun; for the Lord God giveth them light: and they shall reign for ever and ever.

6 And he said unto me, These sayings *are* faithful and true: and the Lord God of the holy prophets sent his angel to shew unto his servants the things which must shortly be done.

Revelation is written *to the servants of God,* that is, *all* Christians.

7 Behold, I come quickly: blessed *is* he that keepeth the sayings of the prophecy of this book.

8 And I John saw these things, and heard *them.* And when I had heard and seen, I fell down to worship before the feet of the angel which shewed me these things.

9 Then saith he unto me, See *thou do it* not: for I am thy fellow servant, and of thy brethren the prophets, and of them which keep the sayings of this book: worship God.

10 And he saith unto me, Seal not the sayings of the prophecy of this book: for the time is at hand.

11 He that is unjust, let him be unjust still: and he which is filthy, let him be filthy still: and he that is righteous, let him be righteous still: and he that is holy, let him be holy still.

12 And, behold, I come quickly; and my reward *is* with me, to give every man according as his work shall be.

13 I am Alpha and Omega, the beginning and the end, the first and the last.

14 Blessed *are* they that do his commandments, that they may have right to the tree of life, and may enter in through the gates into the city.

15 For without are dogs, and sorcerers, and whoremongers, and murderers, and idolaters, and whosoever loveth and maketh a lie.

Dogs represent the "filthy" in verse eleven. Dogs were considered unclean in the East, because they wandered streets and fields and would eat dead bodies. Cities kept the dogs out because nothing unclean was allowed to enter. Unclean sinners, likewise, will never enter God's holy city.

16 I Jesus have sent mine angel to testify unto you these things in the churches. I am the root and the offspring of David, *and* the bright and morning star.
17 And the Spirit and the bride say, Come. And let him that heareth say, Come. And let him that is athirst come. And whosoever will, let him take the water of life freely.

Let's get out and witness. Say to sinners, "*Come* to God." Pray daily, "Thy kingdom *come*." Come, Lord Jesus.

18 For I testify unto every man that heareth the words of the prophecy of this book, If any man shall add unto these things, God shall add unto him the plagues that are written in this book:
19 And if any man shall take away from the words of the book of this prophecy, God shall take away his part out of the book of life, and out of the holy city, and *from* the things which are written in this book.

Those are serious and eternally consequential warnings. We must handle the Word of God with fear and trembling. Let God be true and every man a liar.

20 He which testifieth these things saith, Surely I come quickly. Amen. Even so, come, Lord Jesus.

None of us are promised a tomorrow. *Today* is the day to serve the King of kings. It's all or nothing. Are you in?

21 The grace of our Lord Jesus Christ *be* with you all. Amen.

Final Words and Encouragement

P lease do not avoid or delay turning to God with your whole heart, in faith and with a lowly heart of repentance. Our Lord has patiently waited "a thousand years" for the harvest of the earth, his eternal family. He takes no pleasure in the eternal destruction of the unrighteous. God's judgment is holy and righteous. Those who will be cast into the devil's hell are unredeemable and will have shunned numerous calls for God's grace and mercy. God knows every one of us, inside and out. Don't fear. Come to Him and trust Him with the rest of your days. He will never disappoint you. The rewards will be eternal.

The Day of the Lord—That Day

Zephaniah 1:1–18

1 This is the word of the LORD that came to Zephaniah son of Cushi, the son of Gedaliah, the son of Amariah, the son of Hezekiah, in the days of Josiah son of Amon king of Judah:

2 "I will completely sweep away **everything** from the face of the earth," declares the LORD.

3 "I will sweep away **man and beast**; I will sweep away the birds of the air, and the fish of the sea, and the idols with their

wicked worshipers. I will cut off mankind from the face of the earth," declares the LORD.

4 "I will stretch out My hand against Judah and against all who dwell in Jerusalem. I will cut off from this place every remnant of Baal, the names of the idolatrous and pagan priests—

5 those who bow on the rooftops to worship the host of heaven, those who bow down and swear by the LORD but also swear by Milcom,

6 and those who turn back from following the LORD, neither seeking the LORD nor inquiring of Him."

7 Be silent in the presence of the Lord GOD, for **the Day** of the LORD is near. Indeed, the LORD has prepared a sacrifice; He has consecrated His guests.

8 "On **the Day** of the LORD's sacrifice I will punish the princes, the sons of the king, and all who are dressed in foreign apparel.

9 On **that day** I will punish all who leap over the threshold, who fill the house of their master with violence and deceit.

10 On **that day**," declares the LORD, "a cry will go up from the Fish Gate, a wail from the Second District, and a loud crashing from the hills.

11 Wail, O dwellers of the Hollow, for all your merchants will be silenced; all who weigh out silver will be cut off.

12 And **at that time** I will search Jerusalem with lamps and punish the men settled in complacency, who say to themselves, 'The LORD will do nothing, either good or bad.'

13 Their wealth will be plundered and their houses laid waste. They will build houses but not inhabit them, and plant vineyards but never drink their wine.

14 **The great Day** of the LORD is near—near and coming quickly. Listen, **the Day** of the LORD. Then the cry of the mighty will be bitter.

15 **That day** will be **a day** of wrath, **a day** of trouble and distress, **a day** of destruction and desolation, **a day** of darkness and gloom, **a day** of clouds and blackness,

16 **a day** of horn blast and battle cry against the fortified cities, and against the high corner towers.

17 I will bring such distress on mankind that they will walk like the blind, because they have sinned against the LORD. Their blood will be poured out like dust and their flesh like dung.

18 Neither their silver nor their gold will be able to deliver them on **the Day** of the LORD's wrath. **The whole earth** will be consumed by the fire of His jealousy." For indeed, He will make **a sudden end** of **all who dwell on the earth**. (**Berean Study Bible**)

The Great Day of the Lord's Vengeance
is very near!
Few today understand
that we are at the very end
of the Lord's patience and restraint
toward the gross wickedness
of mankind on the earth.

~

Today is the day
to be certain of your
salvation!

Dear Jesus,

I want to make the necessary changes in my life because I want to be in right relationship with You. I need You to take the reigns of my life. I do not want to be separated from You for

eternity. Please forgive me for my sin, and do whatever work needs to be done in me to make me Your faithful follower.

In Your name I pray.
Amen.

Endnotes

1   https://Biblehub.com/commentaries/pulpit/revelation/11.htm

2   https://www.opendoorsusa.org/christian-persecution/stories/christian-persecution-by-the-numbers/

3   https://www.christianity.com/Bible/commentary.php?com=mhc&b=66&c=3

4   https://Biblehub.com/commentaries/pulpit/zechariah/4.htm

5   https://Biblehub.com/commentaries/revelation/12–15.htm

6   https://Biblehub.com/sermons/auth/seiss/the_144000.htm

CPSIA information can be obtained
at www.ICGtesting.com
Printed in the USA
BVHW080117070421
604328BV00006B/72